The Ajanta Caves

Kate,

We discovered a way to share a bit of our trip with you - Thanks for your care that makes certain we can enjoy these caves, this fabulous trip -

Sally + Paul

The Ajanta Caves

Artistic Wonder of Ancient Buddhist India

Text and Photographs by Benoy K. Behl

With additional notes on the *Jataka* stories by Sangitika Nigam

Foreword by Milo C. Beach

Harry N. Abrams, Inc., Publishers

To my father, Manthar Krishen Behl,

whose rational thinking and sensitive humanity

have constantly inspired me.

The line drawings that appear on pp. 13, 32, 36, 38, and 60–2, are reproduced from A. Ghosh (ed.), *Ajanta Murals* (Delhi, 1967), by kind permission of the Director-General of the Archaeological Survey of India. The cave plans on pp. 26 and 234–7 are reproduced from Madanjeet Singh, *The Cave Paintings of Ajanta* (London, 1965), by courtesy of the author.

Library of Congress Cataloging-in-Publication Data

Behl, Benoy K., 1956–
The Ajanta caves : artistic wonder of ancient Buddhist India / by
Benoy K. Behl; with additional texts on the jataka stories by Sangitika
Nigam; foreword by Milo C. Beach.
          p.   cm.
    Includes bibliographical references and index.
    ISBN 0-8109-1983-4 (clothbound)
    1. Mural painting and decoration, Buddhist—India—Ajanta.
2. Mural painting and decoration, Indic—India—Ajanta.   3. Gautama
Buddha—Art.   4. Cave temples, Buddhist—India—Ajanta.   5. Cave
temples—India—Ajanta.   6. Ajanta Caves (India)   I. Nigam, Sangitika.
II. Title.
ND2829.A4B44   1998
751.7 3 095484—dc21   97-32237

Introduction and photographs copyright © 1998 Benoy K. Behl

First published in Great Britain in 1998 by Thames and Hudson Ltd., London

Published in 1998 by Harry N. Abrams, Incorporated, New York

Printed and bound in Singapore

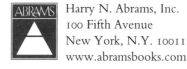

Harry N. Abrams, Inc.
100 Fifth Avenue
New York, N.Y. 10011
www.abramsbooks.com

CONTENTS

PREFACE AND ACKNOWLEDGMENTS

This book on the artistic legacy of Ajanta is the result of a long labour of love. In retrospect it seems so strange that the undertaking really began as a mainly technical exercise of photographing the priceless heritage of these paintings, which had not been accurately reproduced before because of restrictions in the use of artificial lighting in the cave interiors. On the very first day, however, as I stood in front of an image of the Buddha in Cave 26, everything was changed.

The compassion and humility of the artists of a long-gone era are clearly evident in the masterpieces which they created, and I was captivated by them. The long days spent before the profusion of mural paintings taught me, in every moment, about the tradition of reverential dedication which guided the hands of the artists. In a simple and small way, by documenting this noble work, I felt connected to a great tradition.

This book will, I hope, bring the exquisite paintings of Ajanta to a wide range of discerning viewers and help to establish even more firmly the place of this priceless inheritance in the art traditions of the world. I take this opportunity to thank those who, through their individual appreciation and encouragement, helped to make this venture possible. First of all, my deepest gratitude is owed to Mr M.C. Joshi, who was then Director-General of the Archaeological Survey of India, for giving me permission in 1991 to photograph the paintings and for his most generous response to the results of the documentation. Dr Kapila Vatsayan, who saw the first results the very next day, was extremely encouraging in her appreciation. Dr Peter L.M. Heydemann, then Senior Counsellor for Science and Technology at the United States Embassy in New Delhi, responded with keen interest to the technological breakthrough achieved by my use of long exposures in dim light and to the beauty of the resulting images, and he very kindly introduced my work to experts in the USA. I am deeply grateful to him for his continued support and generous friendship.

I am also greatly indebted to Mr Sadashiv Gorakshkar, then Director of the Prince of Wales Museum of Western India in Bombay, and to Dr Kalpana Desai, who were very enthusiastic in their response to the photography. The former was very generous in his view that the paintings of Ajanta would be reappraised in the light of the reproductions now made available, while the personal encouragement of Dr Desai motivated me to take up the writing of the present book as soon as possible. My thanks are also owed to Mrs Phiroza Godrej, who came forward very helpfully to hold the first exhibition of my photographs at her Cymroza Art Gallery in Mumbai, and to His Excellency Dr P.C. Alexander, Governor of Maharashtra, who inaugurated the display with generous words of encouragement. I am immensely grateful to Dr Alexander for his support and to Mrs Ackama Alexander, who very kindly released the catalogue of the exhibition.

My gratitude is especially owed to two eminent scholars who knew Ajanta so well: the late Dr Stella Kramrisch, who kindly invited me to the Philadelphia Museum of Art to show my work there, and the late Mr Karl Khandalawala, who was very warmly appreciative. I am deeply indebted to Dr Milo C. Beach, Director of the Freer Gallery of Art and the Arthur M. Sackler Gallery, Smithsonian Institution, Washington, D.C., who has a rich and broad understanding of Asian art and painting. His positive and valued response to my work at Ajanta, as well as to my photographs of the Brhadisvara temple paintings, has been immensely encouraging. I am also grateful to Dr Beach for having kindly contributed the Foreword to this book, placing Ajanta in the context of its importance as a fountainhead of Buddhist artistic traditions throughout Asia. Professor Michael Meister, Chair of Fine Arts at the University of Pennsylvania, Professor Ikuo Hirayama, President of the Tokyo National University of Fine Arts & Music, Dr Pratapaditya Pal of the Los Angeles County Museum of Art, Dr Ellen Smart of the San Diego Museum of Art, Dr Rajeshwari Ghose of Hong Kong University, and Dr M.A. Dhaky, whose scholarship I deeply respect, have given me their most helpful support and I owe to them my heartfelt thanks.

The Ajanta photography and also the on-going documentation of the tradition of Indian painting and of other cultural sites in Asia have been very kindly commented upon and encouraged by some of the finest writers and critics, including Ms Amita Malik, Mr Khushwant Singh and Mr Dom Moraes, and I am grateful to them for having again brought Ajanta to the forefront of critical interest in India. Ms Roshan Shahani, Ms Sumitra Kumar Srinivasan, Ms Manisha Pandey-Thakur, Mr A. Mahadevan and Mr Amit Prakash, as well as other writers, have also played a vital role in introducing the art of Ajanta to a wide range of people in India and helped create an awareness of the imperative need to preserve this great artistic legacy. My sincerest thanks are extended to them.

This long and exciting journey of discovering and documenting India's diverse cultural roots has been possible, despite the many trials encountered in dealing with the vastness of the subject and the difficulties of working in remote areas, thanks to the constant warmth and inspiring support of my dear friends Anil Saari, Madhukar Upadhyay, Subroto Sen, James and Praveen Lyngdoh, Lekha Poddar, Geetha and M.R. Srinivasan, Chiranjiv Singh, Ken and Mary Brill, Sitakant Mahapatra, Nirupama Rao, Ashok Vajpeyi, Chuden Tsering Misra, Premlata Puri, Pradeep Mehendiratta, Sridhar Iyengar, Francine Berkowitz, Inder Pasricha, Usha Balakrishnan, R.K.Vishwanathan and many others.

My very special thanks go to Dr R. Chidambaram, Chairman of the Indian Atomic Energy Commission, Mr B.P. Singh, Secretary, Department of Culture, Government of India, Mr M.P. Bezbaruah, Secretary, Department of Tourism, Government of India, Mr Ajai Shankar, Director-General of the Archaeological Survey of India, and Dr Aruna Bagchi, Secretary of Tourism, Government of Maharashtra, to whom I am indebted for encouragement and support in making it possible for me to carry out further work in the field and who are making valuable contributions to the conservation of the Ajanta caves and other heritage monuments which have been documented in recent years.

My warm thanks also go to my secretary Valerie D'Silva and assistant Uday Bandarkar, who have worked long and late hours in fulfilling the numerous tasks involved in the preparation of this book.

The loving encouragement constantly given to me by my dear parents has been a tremendous support during the lengthy periods devoted to my research into and photographing of the Ajanta caves. Finally, this work would not have been possible without the patience and dedication of Sangitika Nigam, my friend and associate in carrying out the research and fieldwork.

BENOY K. BEHL

FOREWORD

A visit to the Buddhist site of Ajanta is one of the great human experiences. An unforgettable drama unfolds as one leaves behind the sun-filled gorge of the Waghora River to enter the intense dark interiors of those vast man-made caves. The initial disorientation quickens the senses, but it is only very slowly that the eyes can adapt and respond; after some time, carved forms and painted walls begin to emerge from the blackness. Buddhas, Bodhisattvas, palaces inhabited by women of extraordinary sensuousness, musicians, lotus ponds – the entire panoply of the natural world eventually takes on vital visual life. The emergence of such energy from what initially had seemed empty darkness is deeply symbolic, of course. It demands the visitor's time and patience. A true appreciation of it also demands an actual visit.

The varieties and qualities of light and darkness are extraordinarily important at Ajanta. On occasion sections of the major caves have been artificially illuminated with a low level of electric lighting or by hand-held flashlights, while others have sunlight directed into the interiors off reflective surfaces held by guides standing outside the entrances (in each case sections of the imagery are isolated and the colour of the wall surface is distorted in illuminated areas). If one explores the site thoroughly, one finds that the majority of the caves remain almost completely dark, for the entrances are small and natural light seldom travels far within. Only in these conditions can the modern visitor come to sense the daily experience of the people for whom the caves were made. Originally any light must have come from small oil lamps which could only have served to intensify a mysterious and unearthly effect.

One reason why Benoy Behl's photographs are so successful is that his working method recognizes and respects the visual experience of those who originally worshipped at the caves. Rather than invading the spaces and snatching artificially illuminated details, his camera slowly gathers natural light, recreating the experience of the human worshipper's eye. His images allow the caves to speak for themselves, and the result is a level of sensitivity, and of truth to texture, colour and effect that is without precedent. His photographs bring us closer to direct experience of being at Ajanta than has ever before been possible, and his work will certainly inspire renewed interest in a site that remains crucially important to the understanding of Buddhist art throughout Asia.

Ajanta, for example, provides virtually the only remaining evidence of styles of painting that first developed in India and then travelled with Buddhism into the Himalayan regions and then, via the Silk Roads, across Central Asia into China, Japan and Korea. Here, the artistic creations, dating from a period when certain schools of Buddhism were just beginning to invent architectural forms and imagery appropriate to their beliefs, include nothing that has been repeated by rote; throughout, the art of Ajanta reveals the freshness of new invention, and it stands virtually alone in its ability to illuminate these early periods of a pan-Asian development. Benoy Behl's photographs are a worthy tribute to one of the greatest cultural sites in Asia.

MILO CLEVELAND BEACH

INTRODUCTION

'Beauty is truth, truth beauty,' – that is all
Ye know on earth, and all ye need to know.

JOHN KEATS (1795–1821), 'Ode on a Grecian Urn'

When one is present at the rock-cut Buddhist caves of Ajanta in Western India, completely enraptured in the world of its paintings, one is reminded of these words of Keats. Indeed – for all the historical importance of the paintings of Ajanta, for all the doctrine of Buddhism, as it evolved through hundreds of years, for all the surprising and immensely sophisticated stylistic and technical developments in painting of which Ajanta represents the sole surviving inheritance – one cannot help but be completely immersed in the sheer beauty, both pictorial and emotive, that is presented here. Along with but above all scholarly considerations, a relationship with Ajanta is always one of the heart. It is impossible, even in a brief encounter with the atmospheric world of the Ajanta caves, not to experience a deep and marvellous emotional thrill. Indeed, the artists of many centuries ago still manage to convey their original meaningful message to the sensitive viewer of today.

We are reminded of the fact that the Philosophy of Aesthetics was highly developed in very early times in India, long before the beginning of the Christian Era. There is a considerable amount of textual material recording the extensive debates since those times on the subject of the importance of aesthetics: about why beautiful temples, sculptures and paintings should be made. The Indian philosopher concludes that the state of 'ecstasy' (Greek, a state in which the soul has come out of the physical body, and is therefore in closer union with the rest of Creation – a state for which, in Indian and many other philosophies, the soul is constantly yearning) which is experienced on seeing a beautiful sunrise or an exquisite painting is close to 'Brahmananda' (the final joy of supreme knowledge). As supreme knowledge may be attained by only very few and then only after considerable years of having 'wept and fasted, wept and prayed', this other path which brings the human soul, from time to time, into a tangible contact with the greater bliss through the aesthetic experience, found a prominent place and importance among the many tributaries of the broad stream of Indian philosophy.

A dedicatory inscription of the fifth century AD in Cave 27 at Ajanta reads:

> May this Hall, out of affection. . . . cause the attainment of well-being for good people as
> long as the sun dispels darkness by its rays!
>
> (translated by Dr V.V. Mirashi)

and the beneficial effects of art are summed up in the treatise on painting entitled *The Vishnudharmottara* (*Chitrasutra*, ch. 43):

> A painting cleanses and curbs anxiety, augments future good, causes unequalled and pure
> delight, kills the evil spirits of bad dreams and pleases the household deity.
>
> (translated by Dr Stella Kramrisch).

THE COMPASSIONATE WORLD OF BUDDHISM

The paintings of the ancient rock-cut caves of Ajanta exquisitely enshrine a compassionate view of life. They are the work of devout artists, whose themes are Buddhist, but they reflect a sublime religiosity which knows no bounds between different faiths. It is quite certain that the artists who painted these caves were members of guilds and would also have painted themes associated with other faiths.

On the walls of Ajanta, there is no creature, however humble or glorious, be it an ant or a prince, that does not receive the attention and reverential touch of the painter. The men and women who inhabit this world of compassion have the capacity to adore, and the artists who created the murals convey such feelings in graphic detail. Thus, within the *Jataka* narrative scenes (in which stories of the Lord Buddha in his previous births in both human and various animal forms are depicted) the beings are shown looking upon each other with expressions of infinite caring.

These sentiments are suggested by the attitudes of listening: people are seen to be concerned about what happens to others. There is the exchange of looks, warm and caring. There is also the directness of the gentle human touch, expressed in a manner which is largely lost in modern society, as we see in the scene showing palace maids commiserating with each other as they share their deep sorrow at the news that King Mahajanaka has resolved to abandon the worldly life (p. 88).

Another aspect is the inward look: the 'Bodhisattvas' (previous births of Lord Buddha / beings on the path to Enlightenment) are painted with all the activity of everyday life around them, yet they look within. It is this life of spiritual beings that pervades the world depicted in these paintings.

Individual artists may or may not be Buddhists, but each is a *bhikshu* (one who has renounced the worldly life to pursue his spiritual search as a homeless wanderer in the Indian tradition). Hence, he is humble before all the creatures of the Lord. In the world of Ajanta, even the great and glorious King Mahajanaka kneels and folds his hands before the hermit, with a look of adoration upon his face (p. 87).

If after viewing these paintings one comes away from Ajanta with a little more of the capacity within one's breast to adore another living being – then the *bhikshu* has succeeded in reaching across to us over all those hundreds of years, and has shared the breath of his devotion with us.

The Buddha preaching after his descent from the Tushita Heaven: his words are heard in an atmosphere of devout reverence, by groups of seated noblemen on the left and monks on the right. This scene is painted on the left-hand wall of the antechamber of the shrine in Cave 17 (see p. 204).

THE SITE OF THE CAVES

> (There) was a mountain range, ridges one above another in succession, tiers of peaks and sheer summits. Here was a monastery . . . its lofty halls and deep chambers were quarried in the cliff.

Thus wrote Hsuan T'sang, the Chinese pilgrim of the early seventh century AD in describing Ajanta. His is the first known literary reference to the caves.

Here, carved deep into the living rock, are stupendous monuments to man's religious zeal, artistic creations which, as the cave inscriptions proclaim, were intended to last for ever. The ancient site consists of 31 caves which were excavated in two distinct phases in the horseshoe-shaped gorge of the Waghora River in the Sahyadri Hills in the Aurangabad district of Maharashtra in Western India (p. 17). In this wild solitude, amid forests and age-less hills, the followers of the Buddha sought spiritual solace. They created an isolated haven, far from worldly thought, in which to meditate in peace.

In 1819, a party of British soldiers on a hunting expedition chanced upon the Ajanta caves. The site was named after the village of Ajintha which is situated about 3 miles (5 km) distant as the crow flies. The exquisite mural paintings found here, shrouded in the darkness of the caves, were considered by those who rediscovered them to be in every respect as beautiful as much later European paintings of the thirteenth and fourteenth centuries. Indeed, Ajanta was an amazing find in the history of world art.

This enchanted place has been designated a World Heritage Site by UNESCO. The caves are numbered not chronologically, but serially from the entrance to the site at the east end along the rock face of 600 yards (550 metres). There is evidence that individual caves would once have had stairways leading down to the River Waghora below. Almost all the original steps have since collapsed and are gone. Only a few steps have survived, such as those in front of the centrally situated Cave 16, but these give us an idea of the original relationship of the caves to the river. Today, a terraced path of modern construction takes the visitor along the horseshoe bend of the site (see plan opposite).

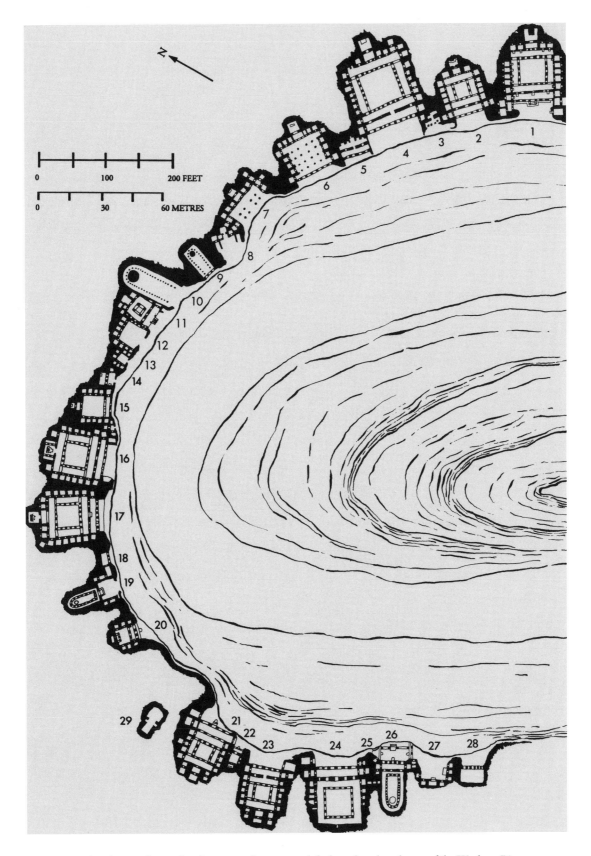

Site plan showing the numbered sequence of caves around the horseshoe-shaped gorge of the Waghora River.

OPPOSITE: *Remoteness and the natural grandeur of the sight were key reasons for the early Buddhists' choice of Ajanta for their rock-cut caves, where they could meditate in peace. Their prayer halls and sanctuaries could be approached only on foot from the east, by passing along the lower levels of the gorge created by the Waghora River. Here, the river forms a horseshoe-shaped bend (top right). The sheer face of the rock is punctuated by several waterfalls which, during the monsoon season, produce cascades as they plunge down from the surrounding plateau. The Waghora descends in seven leaps or cascades called 'Sat-kund' (top left). A partial view of the side of the gorge seen from the south (centre) shows several of the rock-cut façades, from the two-storey Cave 6 on the left to Cave 1 on the right. Buddhist monks, who survived by collecting alms, came here to take shelter in the caves during the monsoons.*

Among the caves that feature striking sculptures are two chaityas or prayer halls (bottom): the entrance façade of Cave 9, one of the earliest excavations dating from the second century BC, with a much later figure of the Buddha depicted in the Abhaya mudra posture, granting fearlessness to his followers; and the unfinished Cave 26, dating from the sixth century AD, the interior of which features elaborate, finely carved friezes depicting the Buddha and his attendants.

Two contrasting sculptural themes in Cave 1 reveal the diversity of subject matter and the range of skills and imaginative treatment displayed by the artists of Ajanta.

ABOVE: *A detail from the friezes decorating the façade, in which scenes from the life of the Buddha are depicted. Here, the young Prince Siddhartha rides out of the royal palace in a chariot; on the left he witnesses the corpse of a dead man being borne* *away to be cremated, while on the right he looks out at an aged man who is in a pitiable state. These scenes represent two of the Ominous Sights that led the prince to recognize the futility of worldly existence, which he later renounced.*

ABOVE: *Inside the main hall on the right-hand side one of the capitals is subtly carved to create the illusion of four recumbent and standing deer sharing a single head.*

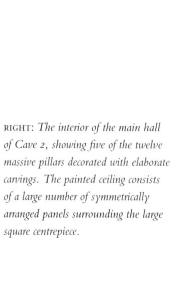

RIGHT: *The interior of the main hall of Cave 2, showing five of the twelve massive pillars decorated with elaborate carvings. The painted ceiling consists of a large number of symmetrically arranged panels surrounding the large square centrepiece.*

Cave 4

The shrine within this cave contains a large figure of the Buddha, shown seated in the teaching posture (opposite). The two deer placed in front of him symbolize the First Sermon delivered by the Buddha at Sarnath, when he set in motion the Wheel of Dharma. Flanking the Buddha are figures of the Bodhisattvas Padmapani and Avalokitesvara.

Sculpted in the verandah, to the right of the entrance, is a very early depiction of the Lord of Compassion, the Bodhisattva Avalokitesvara, with a long-stemmed lotus in his hand (damaged now). He is represented as the saviour of mankind, threatened by the Eight Great Perils: an Elephant, a Lion, a Snake, a Robber, Fire, Water, Fetters and a Demon.

Among the sculpted figures that decorate the capitals of columns in the hall are musicians playing stringed instruments. Here, the instrument is similar in form to a mandolin. Such figures provide us with many valuable insights into the everyday activities of contemporary society.

Cave 6

This cave, dating from the fifth–sixth centuries, features an upper and a lower floor, the only example of a double-storeyed cave at Ajanta.

On each floor the walls of the antechamber to the main shrine are elaborately carved with sculptures, some of which retain traces of the original paint (left). The left-hand side of the antechamber to the main shrine at the lower level is decorated with a painting, now partially destroyed, of the Buddha in the teaching posture (opposite). He is shown seated on a lotus and surrounded by attendants and worshippers.

Cave 6

In the antechamber to the shrine in the upper storey, a bhikshu *is depicted on the left kneeling before a large statue of the Buddha. In his right hand he holds a censer, and with his left hand he proffers lotuses to the Enlightened One; the three blooms symbolize the Buddha, the Order and the Law, known collectively as the* Triratna *(Three Jewels).*

THE EARLY HINAYANA PHASE

The caves of the earlier phase at Ajanta date from around the second century BC, during the rule of the Satavahana dynasty. Although the Satavahanas were Hindu rulers, they were tolerant towards Buddhism. During the period of their rule there was political stability in the area, and this led to the promotion of extensive trade and commerce within the land and with the Mediterranean world. This in turn created the wealth which gave a tremendous fillip to the arts of that period. It is also important to remember that the Ajanta caves and hundreds of other rock-cut sites in Western India lay along trade routes and must certainly have provided shelter to the itinerant merchants of those times. Some of these merchants in fact contributed to the making of these caves (a very early inscription in Cave 12 states that it was the gift of a merchant named Ghanamadada.)

The early caves of Ajanta were made by the Hinayana Buddhists. This is the oldest form of Buddhism, which does not allow any representations of the Buddha. He was worshipped through symbols and ritual mounds called stupas. Two of these ancient caves are *chaityas* (prayer halls); they are numbered 9 and 10 in the sequence. The others are *viharas* (monasteries for monks to live in), numbered 8, 12, 13 and 15A. Originally, all the surfaces of the walls and ceilings of the caves must have been painted. Today, however, beautiful murals survive in only a few of these early caves. One feels a sense of awe when looking at the remnants of the paintings in the two *chaityas* (Caves 9 and 10). Though little now survives of these paintings, they are invaluable as the oldest extant paintings dating from the historical period.

Plans of two of the earliest caves dating from the second century BC, numbered 10 and 9 respectively in the modern system. Both are chaityas, *or prayer halls, with a dominant stupa at the rear; depictions of the Buddha occur only in later caves.*

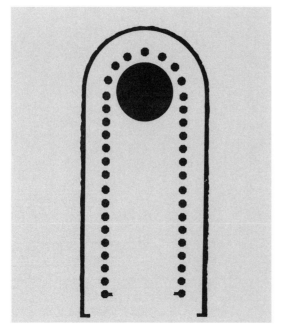
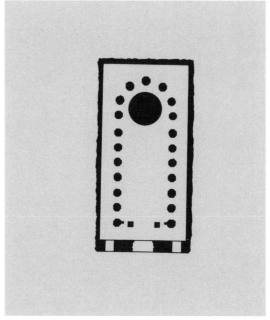

The coiffures and the clothes worn by the figures depicted in these paintings are very similar to those occurring in the early sculpted Buddhist sites of Sanchi and Bharhut; this resemblance helps us to date the original paintings to the second–first centuries BC. Caves 9 and 10 also feature later paintings made over the earlier Hinayana murals, such as the one-eyed monk before the Buddha (p. 43).

In Cave 10 is the signature inscribed by John Smith on 28 April 1819, when he and his party of British soldiers, while out on a hunting expedition, chanced upon the caves. On the walls and the pillars of this cave there are many donative inscriptions by monks who must have provided for the paintings. For example, on the left wall, opposite the space between the fifth and sixth pillars, an inscription reads: 'The meritorious gift of the teacher . . . Sachiva. Whatever merit is in this let that be for [the good of] all sentient beings.' This inscription, like numerous others at Ajanta, demonstrates the quality of humanity and compassion of a faith which encompasses in its generous charity the benefit not only of mankind but of all living things.

THE SECOND CREATIVE PHASE

Six centuries after the Hinayana caves were excavated, the Ajanta site witnessed a fresh burst of creative activity. There are numerous Mahayana *viharas* of this period, especially Caves 1, 2, 16 and 17, in which beautiful murals still survive. Two *chaityas* of this period, numbered 19 and 26 respectively, are exquisitely sculpted. These caves, which are among the most beautiful at Ajanta, were excavated and painted in the fifth and sixth centuries AD, under the benevolent rule of the Hindu Vakataka kings. An inscription in Cave 16 states that Varahadeva, minister of King Harisena (*c.* 475–500), dedicated the cave to the Buddhist *sangha* or congregation :

> (May) this mountain, the peak of which contains various caves,
> which is inhabited by great people . . . and may the whole world also,
> getting rid of its manifold sins, enter that tranquil and noble state,
> free from sorrow and pain!
>
> (translated by Dr V. V. Mirashi)

By this time the Hinayana phase of Buddhism had given way to the Mahayana order. The Buddha was no longer represented only by a symbol. Statues were now made depicting Him in various *mudras* (attitudes, such as those of teaching and of blessing), and a considerable Buddhist pantheon had evolved.

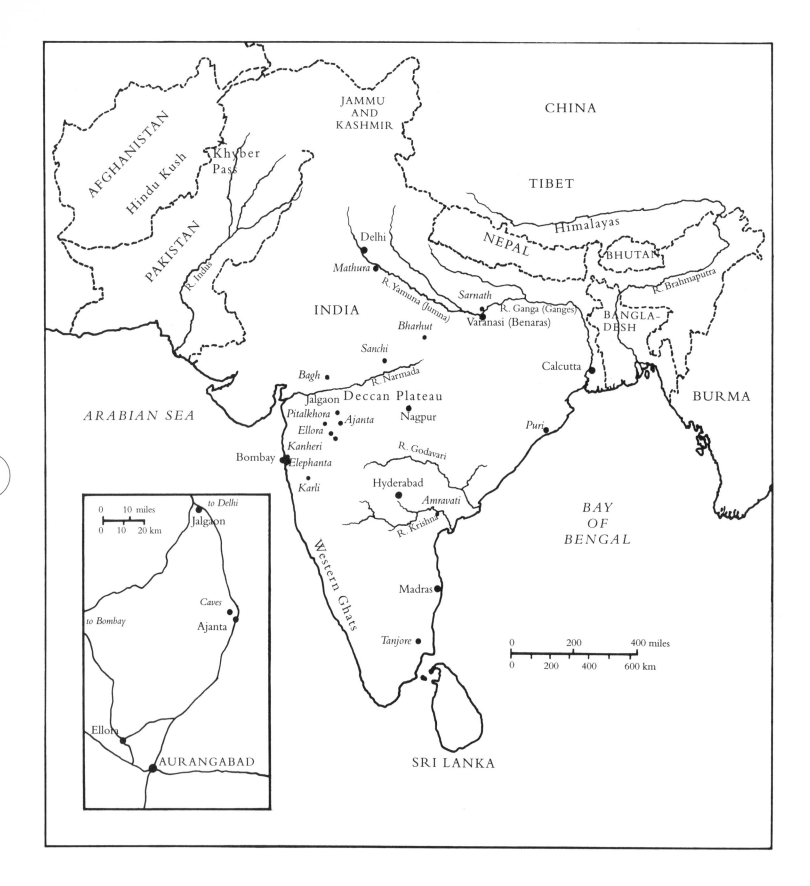

Map of the Indian subcontinent, showing locations of Ajanta and other major early sites (names in italics). The inset shows the positions of the caves at Ellora and Ajanta in relation to the nearest main town, Aurangabad.

Many of the murals in Cave 16 have not survived, but what does remain reveals the exquisite quality of the original paintings. In one scene Queen Sundari is shown pining away because her husband King Nanda has abandoned her to become an ascetic. John Griffiths, who devoted thirteen years (from 1872 to 1885) to making reproductions of Ajanta murals, said of this painting (pp. 154–5), which is called the 'Dying Princess': 'For pathos and sentiment and the unmistakable way of telling its story this picture cannot be surpassed in the history of art.'

In Cave 17 there is a surviving inscription which tells us that this magnificent *vihara* was donated by a feudatory of King Harisena:

> While that moon among princes Harisena, whose face resembles a lotus . . . and who does what is beneficial for (his) subjects . . . is protecting the earth . . . (He excavated) this monolithic excellent Hall, containing within a Chaitya of the king of ascetics (the Buddha) and possessing the qualities of stateliness.
>
> (translated by Dr V.V. Mirashi)

This is a beautiful cave, the walls of which are covered with paintings of many *Jataka* stories. The *Simhala Avadana* and the *Visvantara Jataka* depicted here in all the complexity of their numerous incidents, and each occupying about 45 ft (13.75 m) of wall space, are truly magnificent murals conceived on a vast and impressive scale.

Soon after Cave 17 was excavated, the great *vihara* now known as Cave 1 was carved out of the rock. Here, the visitor is transported into a world of loveliness, in which the painters reached the highest standards of achievement in the beauty of line and colour, of *bhava* (the depiction of the emotions) and *lavanya* (the beauty of grace). Every painting in this cave reflects the deep reverence of the painters.

Although there is no dedicatory inscription in Cave 1, the development in the style of painting suggests that it is later than that seen in Caves 16 and 17. Dr Walter Spink of the University of Michigan feels that the cave was a donation of King Harisena. In his book *The Achievement of Ajanta* he writes: 'Ajanta . . . was sponsored by the greatest ruler in the world. Furthermore, Ajanta is by all counts this greatest ruler's greatest monument.' Dr Spink also believes that the twenty-six caves of the second period of Ajanta's excavation – some of them unfinished – were all made within the space of eighteen years. The eminent Indian art historian Karl Khandalavala regards this, however, as a complete misunderstanding of the site's development and of the painstaking traditions of the Indian artists who would have worked over a much longer period on the excavation, sculpture and paintings of these caves. In the absence of any conclusive inscriptions, my own understanding is that work on the caves, with their wonderfully chiselled figures and lovingly painted walls and ceilings, would have taken a much longer period of time than that suggested by Dr Spink. Furthermore, if Cave 1 was indeed made at the instance of King Harisena, it is also uncharacteristic of the inscriptions found elsewhere on the site that, though Harisena is spoken of often and described as a 'moon among princes', even his own minister Varahadeva makes no mention of the king having also sponsored the excavation of a cave. Many patrons, including a feudatory of Harisena, the minister Varahadeva, numerous Buddhist monks, a merchant and others have left behind numerous dedicatory inscriptions describing their own efforts. In Dr V.V. Mirashi's translation, the inscription of the monk Buddhabhadra reads: 'A man continues to enjoy himself in paradise as long as his memory is green in the world. One should set up a memorial on the mountains that will endure for as long as the moon and the sun continue.' If such was the belief, it seems virtually certain that either the king himself or his minister, who refers to him at great length, would have stated that the king personally donated one of the major caves.

WORKING METHODS AND SCALE

The unfinished caves at the site provide a very good understanding of how excavations were carried out, working from the ceiling downwards and from the front inwards. Traces of painting which are found in these incomplete caves also indicate that the work of the chisel and of the brush proceeded simultaneously. In Cave 26 figures are outlined in red ochre as preparatory sketches for paintings. Another striking feature of the rock-cut

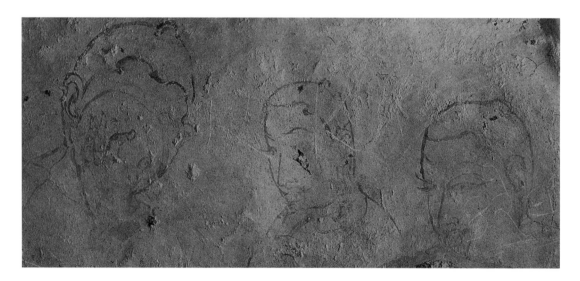

The interior of Cave 26, an unfinished chaitya *dating from the fifth century AD, provides valuable evidence of the artists' working methods. On the left wall are initial sketches, outlined in red ochre, for paintings that were never completed.*

*The magnificent interior of Cave 26, showing the prominent stupa and architectural elements
including ribbing in imitation of roof timbers.*

excavation is the imitation of the wooden buildings of the period. The stone-cutter has carved beams and rafters into the rock, structural elements which are wholly unnecessary in the cave.

The dimensions of the caves vary considerably. Some of the smallest, such as Cave 27, may be considered mere adjuncts of their neighbours. Other caves are hewn out of the rock on a grand scale: Cave 10 is almost 100 ft (30.50 m) long and 40 ft (12.20 m) wide and the main hall alone of Cave 1 is 64 ft (19.50 m) square.

THE NATURE AND SCOPE OF THE MURAL PAINTINGS

The wondrous site of Ajanta is the most beautiful blossoming of Buddhism's art and also represents the last record in the development of this simple and compassionate religion before it lost its warmth and vitality to esoteric and Hindu influences and became a highly organized religious order with a large pantheon of gods and demons.

The paintings that cover the walls of the caves depict stories from the life of the Buddha and the *Jataka* tales (described on pp. 59-62 and in the context of the colour plates). The *Jatakas* are stories of previous births of the Buddha, both as a man and in the form of various animals. Into these parables, which were recounted by the Buddha, are woven the virtuous qualities which he wanted to impress upon his followers. The *Shaddanta Jataka*, for instance, is concerned with the quality of boundless generosity, the *Visvantara Jataka* with the quality of charity and the *Vidhurapandita Jataka* with the quality of wisdom. The depiction of these parables was intended to inculcate in the viewer the idea of leading a virtuous life rather than to impart any religious doctrines or tenets of Buddhism.

The Temptation of the Buddha by Mara: in this scene, painted on the left of the antechamber in Cave 1, the meditating Buddha is not distracted either by the aggressive behaviour of Mara's soldiers or by the charms of his daughters.

A detail from the Shaddanta Jataka *depicted in Cave 17: a row of ants are seen climbing up a branch of a tree (see p. 181)*

The variety of subject-matter in these stories gave the painters ample scope to depict the entire canvas of life on earth. The walls are peopled by men, women and children, rich and poor, in towns and villages, engaged in all kinds of everyday activities. Man is seen here amidst the abundance of Nature, not using her but appearing from among her creatures as the most eloquent form in all creation. In his presentation of the world, the artist of Cave 17 includes even the humble ants, which are depicted on the branch of a tree in the *Shaddanta Jataka* (p. 181).

The themes used in the painted decoration of the ceilings of the caves were in no way religious. The devout visitors would kneel and pray before the religious figures, and this was obviously not practical in the case of images painted on ceilings. Here, the artists give complete freedom and expression to their imagination, painting the familiar animals of the world around them, as well as fantastic and semi-divine creatures derived from all the rich mythology of this land. The painters working at Ajanta felt a close affinity and deep kinship with Nature. They delighted in presenting an endless panorama of flowers, fruits and plants, all held together and unified by a remarkable and highly developed sense of design, which has come to be widely appreciated and admired by modern scholars from all around the world.

He who paints waves, flames, smoke and streamers fluttering in the air, according to the movement of the wind, should be considered a great painter. He knows 'chitra' . . . who [represents] the dead devoid of life movement and the sleeping possessed of it.

(*Vishnudharmottara*, ch. 43, v. 28, translated by Dr Stella Kramrisch, from *The Vishnudharmottara* (Part III), *A Treatise on Indian Painting and Image-making*, Calcutta University Press, 1928)

Of all arts the best is Chitra. It gives the fruit of Dharma, Artha, Kama and Moksha. Wherever it is established in a house, it is the harbinger of the best of auspiciousness.

(*Vishnudharmottara*, ch. 43, v. 38, translated by Dr C. Sivaramamurti, from *Chitrasutra of the Vishnudharmottara*, Kanak Publications, New Delhi, 1978)

By the time of the exquisite second phase of Ajanta, the art of painting was very highly developed in India. Not only were the most beautiful murals executed, as we see in the splendorous walls of Ajanta, but around the same time a marvellous treatise on painting was written: the *Chitrasutra* of the *Vishnudharmottara Purana*. This fascinating document, which includes thousands of guidelines on how to paint, must have been developed for the use of the members of guilds of painters. The treatise provides exhaustive details of methods used in the rendering of different kinds of people, animals and landscapes; three different ways of carrying out shading; instructions on ways of using colour and even on how to prepare colours. From these descriptions we learn that the artist would have spent many days and sometimes even weeks just in preparing the paints which were to be used in the caves. One may well imagine that, after such pains taken by each artist in the preparation of his materials, putting the colours on the walls would have been regarded by him as an act of devotion.

We may sometimes be surprised by the degree of clarity and scientific understanding displayed in this ancient treatise on painting. As an instance, the artist is told that, 'The untrue colour of water resembles that of lapis lazuli. It is the effect of the reflection of the sky in water. But the natural colour of water is seen in the falling down of water-falls; it resembles moonlight.' (translated by Dr Stella Kramrisch). Thus we see the painter working within a long tradition of his art and provided with numerous instructions on how to paint. He is even informed of the relative measurements of different parts of the bodies of human beings from different lands and of different temperaments. Yet, amidst the complex rules framed over the years, it was the breath of inspiration in the individual artists at Ajanta that gave them the freedom to convey their feelings most eloquently. The conventions of past centuries were at his service but, with the sublime ecstasy of his message, the artist is in command, and the lines flow with a unique vitality and gentleness.

In ancient times the different arts were all seen in the Indian tradition as being deeply interwoven one with another. The painter, for instance, was expected to be familiar with dance, music and sculpture. As in the treatise on theatre called the *Natyashastra*, the painter was also expected to express the different *rasas* or emotions. These are *sringara* (erotic or beautiful), *hasya* (humorous), *karuna* (pathos), *vira* (heroic), *raudra* (anger), *bhayanaka* (fearful), *vibhatsa* (loathsome), *adbhuta* (strange and supernatural) and *santa* (peace).

The artists of Ajanta employed a simple palette consisting of five colours, as prescribed in the ancient treatise: white (*sveta*), derived from lime, kaolin and gypsum; red (*rakta*) and yellow (*pita*), obtained from ochre which was found in the nearby hills; black (*Krshna*) from soot; and green (*harit*), extracted from glauconite, a mineral which was also to be found locally. To these was added, in the second phase of the paintings at Ajanta, the blue of lapis lazuli, which was brought from the north-western frontiers of India. These simple colours were blended to produce the innumerable nuances and shades which are found in the paintings. In the words of the *Vishnudharmottara*, 'It would be impossible to enumerate the mixed colours in this world (which are produced by) the mixture of two or three (primary colours) and through invention of various states or conditions (i.e. shades or tones).' (translated by Dr Stella Kramrisch).

The mural paintings of Ajanta are not frescoes, as they are sometimes mistakenly described, for they were not painted on wet lime plaster. These murals were executed with the use of a binding medium of glue applied to a thin coat of dried lime wash. Below this surface wash were two layers of plaster covering the stone walls. The first was a rough, thick layer of mud, mixed with rock-grit, vegetable fibres, grass and other materials; the second was a finer coat consisting of mud, rock dust or sand and finer vegetable fibres, which provided a smooth surface for the lime wash on which the paintings were made.

The painters of these caves belonged to professional guilds and would also have worked in the temples of other religions, as well as in palaces. Indeed the painter was devout, but his devotion was through his art, not limited by the boundaries of any one faith or religion. As beautifully expressed by Dr C. Sivaramamurti in *The Chitrasutra of the Vishnudharmottara*, 'the painter in India was almost like a yogi lost in his art. . . . He created his masterpieces not in the spirit of imposing his personality on an admiring world with a desire for personal honour and fame, but obliterated himself, almost deriving supreme satisfaction in that his art was an offering to God.'

It is this sense of sublime devotion and humility that flows in the lines of Ajanta's paintings. In the attendant figures of the principal characters, the painter comes closest to

The Bodhisattva Padmapani and the Bodhisattva Vajrapani in Cave 1 (see pp. 66, 69)

portraying himself – reverent and completely given over to adoration of another being. Expressions of adoration are exquisitely depicted: a princely figure looking lovingly at King Mahajanaka as he rides forth (p. 96); the concern felt by the palace maids for Queen Sivali (p. 88); King Mahajanaka looking towards a hermit who is delivering a sermon (p. 87). They all appear in that state of ecstasy when the self is given over to another.

No painter worked singly in any one cave; in practice many worked together or at different times. This is seen in the different styles of individual artists within each cave. In Cave 1 styles range from the elegance of the great 'Bodhisattvas' (pp. 66ff.) and of the *Mahajanaka Jataka* (pp. 84ff.) to the far less refined work in the palace scene on the right-hand wall (p. 106). In Cave 2, in the chapel to the right of the antechamber to the main shrine, a very individualistic style is displayed, different from other paintings in that cave. These slender and well-proportioned figures (pp. 126-7) come very close to the highest classic ideals and are among the most beautiful forms of Ajanta.

The Indian painter strives not merely to depict the shape of things seen, but to infuse the representation with a sense of the quality of life. His concern is not only with the physical world and human form, for in his painting realism is constantly tempered by the breath of the life within. The men and women depicted in the murals of Ajanta constantly look within, and it is the life of the spirit rather than that of worldly existence which pervades these paintings. Accordingly, in his use of brush and line the painter strives to observe and depict physical anatomy, but to present through human figures the message of life. The result is certainly not mere physical representation, but the depiction of feelings and ideas which constantly yearn to reach above themselves to a greater reality. The form and content of Ajanta's paintings are marvellously intertwined in a harmonious embrace which always leads us finally to the Buddha's answer of peace and serenity.

The *Jatakas* depicted on the walls reveal a narrative sequence that runs sometimes from left to right, sometimes from right to left, from top to bottom or from bottom to top, and occasionally an incident is found in a seemingly unrelated place in the overall composition. There are no strict demarcations separating one instant in a story from another, but it is as if each finds an exquisite compositional structure of its own accord. Similarly, the individual *Jatakas* are not formally demarcated, so creating the effect of a unified flow from one story to another.

The unique narrative style of the Ajanta murals results in some most interesting compositions. For example, in the story of the birth of the Buddha (painted on the left-hand wall of Cave 2), the court astrologer Asita seems to lean on himself, back to back, as the story unfolds (see line drawing overleaf). This serves as a reminder that in Indian thought the concept of Time is not seen as a constant progression in which whatever has happened is finally over and left behind. Rather, each moment has a life of its own and does not become less important with the passage of time. For instance, every year when the great epic of the Ramayana is enacted, in the moment towards the end of the performance when the victorious Lord Rama returns to the city of Ayodhya with his wife and brother, the earlier scene in which he was banished from the kingdom is no less alive and real in the mind of the audience. We are reminded of the words of T.S. Eliot who was influenced by Indian thought, 'Time present and time past / Are both perhaps present in time future, / And time future contained in time past /...All time is eternally present.'

There are no true shadows in the paintings at Ajanta, but the most subtle nuances of shading, with almost imperceptible deepening and lightening of the same colour, persuade the eye of the roundedness of forms. Eyelids, the nose, lips and the chin are also skilfully highlighted. The brush-strokes are long and bold, producing a grace and sweep which give Ajanta a unique place in art. The artist displays a command of the technique of foreshortening, which is also mentioned in the *Vishnudharmottara*, and is fully familiar with the

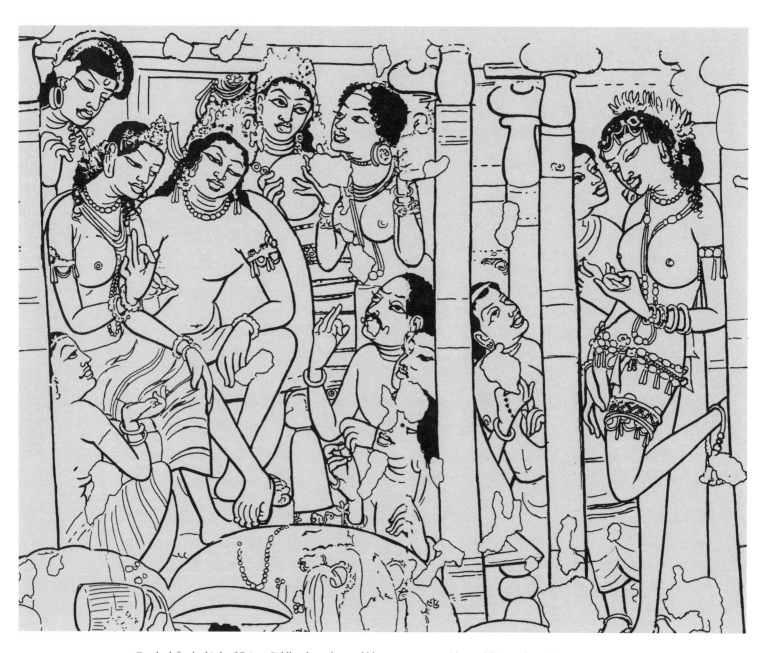

On the left, the birth of Prince Siddhartha, who would become an ascetic (the Buddha), is foretold by the seated court astrologer, Asita, who interprets Queen Mahamaya's dream as she and her husband King Suddhodana listen to his words; on the right, the queen is shown again, deep in thought, as Asita allays her concerns (see p. 122).

principles of perspective. He does not, however, always present scenes in an optically correct perspective, but seeks to show to best effect what is important in any given instant in the scene. Thus, the perspective varies within the painting: often the canopies are shown as if viewed from below (Cave 1, p. 86–7), as they would be seen by the figures in the painting, and the viewer is thus drawn deeper into the drama as the story unfolds. In the same scene from Cave 1, we see other figures brought forward to the viewer's attention through a deliberate reversal of normal perspective. Also, when the Buddha is depicted coming before his wife Yashodhara and son Rahula (Cave 17, p. 200), the application of another canon from the *Vishnudharmottara* is seen: because of his spiritual importance, the Buddha is made to loom large over the other figures.

According to the *Vishnudharmottara*,

> The masters praise the rekhas (delineation and articulation of forms), the connoisseurs praise the display of light and shade, women like the display of ornaments, the rest of the public like richness of colours. Considering this, great care should be taken in the work of chitra, so that, (oh) best of men, it may be appreciated by every one.
>
> (translated by Dr Stella Kramrisch)

The murals of Ajanta are the richest remaining jewel of the ancient art of India. Here the artists lived up to the finest traditions of painting as set forth in the treatise on painting. The caves at Bhaja, Kanheri, Pitalkhora, Bagh and other sites in India were also once profusely painted in this style. Sadly, most of the paintings have been destroyed and little remains to be seen. Paintings dating from the sixth to the tenth centuries are also found at Ellora. The Jain caves at Sittanavasal in Tamil Nadu have beautiful paintings of the ninth century. Another exquisite body of murals is to be found in the inner ambulatory of the tenth-century Brhadisvara temple at Tanjore in South India. At these sites dating from different periods and at others in India may be seen evidence of the remnants of an unbroken tradition of painting from Ajanta in the second century BC onwards.

Cave 9

In this chaitya *of the early period, some murals were overpainted during the second creative phase at Ajanta (fourth-sixth centuries AD). An example is seen in this exquisite detail, which shows a kneeling worshipper – a* sadhu *(ascetic) – with typical hair and beard, just like those of* sadhus *still seen in India today.*

Cave 10

In this early chaitya *dating from the second century BC, the hexagonal pillars are decorated with paintings which must have been executed over existing works several centuries later* in the Mahayana period. Such paintings, as well as sculptures at Ajanta carved during the second major phase of creative activity, reveal stylistic influences of the Indo-Greek art of the Gandhara School, transmitted from the north-west of India.

In the detail shown opposite, a monk – blind in one eye – is depicted paying homage to the seated Buddha, who is seen in the teaching posture. The details of the garments with their flowing forms are skilfully delineated.

Cave 19

This magnificently carved interior (opposite) of this chaitya *dating from the Mahayana period has as its focal point a tall stupa decorated with a standing figure of the Buddha within a monumental arched doorway. The columns surrounding the central open space are surmounted by intricately sculpted capitals and a continuous frieze (above) punctuated by niches containing small figures of the Buddha, alternately standing and seated. The ceiling has been elaborately carved with simulated timber roof supports, in imitation of contemporary architecture.*

Cave 26

In this cave some of the finest sculptures at Ajanta are to be found. On either side of the entrance are figures of beautiful damsels (shalbhanjikas), each holding a branch of the tree under which she stands (opposite); such figures which are frequently seen in doorways, are considered to be auspicious and to symbolize fertility.

Inside the cave is a graphic and sensitive portrayal (right) of the grief of Ananda, one of the closest disciples of the Buddha, at the Parinirvana (see p. 51), when He leaves his mortal body.

OPPOSITE: *In Cave 17, dating from the fifth century AD, is one of the most admired paintings at Ajanta. This beautifully executed portrait, painted on a pilaster separating the front and right aisles, shows a richly bejewelled lady looking into a mirror. Behind her and under her feet can be seen stones and rocky formations depicted in geometric patterns (in accordance with the curious convention that was followed at Ajanta).*

ON THE PRESERVATION OF THE PAINTINGS

The paintings of the Ajanta caves, both those which belong to the second century BC and those of the fifth-sixth centuries AD, have suffered considerably from the ravages of time and also at the hands of misguided visitors who, ever since the caves were rediscovered in the nineteenth century, sometimes removed sections of the murals. Early painters who attempted to make reproductions are also known to have applied varnishes in an attempt to brighten the effect of the paintings, a misguided practice which has led to considerable damage to the murals.

The Nizam of Hyderabad, in whose dominion the caves of Ajanta were situated before he ceded to the Indian Union, called in two Italian restorers who in 1920–21 and 1921–22 made a misguided attempt to preserve the fragile murals. In accordance with the current practice used in preservation at the time, they applied shellac to the surfaces of the paintings. However, with the passage of time the coats of shellac darkened and yellowed. This process led to a distortion of the original colours and to the loss of the subtle nuances and shades which are inherent to the exquisite beauty of the murals. This surface layer also had the effect of attracting soot and other particles, which greatly obscured the paintings in many parts.

Since the Archaeological Survey of India took over the care and conservation of the paintings in the post-Independence period, very considerable effort has been made to remove the damaging layers of shellac as far as can be managed with safety, without harming the original pigments below. In addition, loose plaster on the walls of the caves has been consolidated and damaged areas in the paintings and in the plaster have been fixed using plaster of Paris and cement.

THE SCULPTURES

Ajanta is also one of the most beautiful sites of sculpture in India. The inspired artists who carved out the striking reliefs and figures in the caves do not often receive the fulsome appreciation they deserve, because their work has tended to be overshadowed by the magnificent murals. The sculpture at Ajanta is exceptional for its grace and elegance. It is supple and very expressive.

Notable examples include the impressive and emotive scene of the *Parinirvana* (the Final Renunciation, when the Buddha leaves his mortal body) in Cave 26 and the exquisite Buddha figures in the façade of Cave 19, one of which is shown overleaf. These and other works, such as those illustrated here on pp. 17, 18, 20, 21, 22, 44, 45, 46 and 47,

The famous Parinirvana *scene which occupies most of the length of Cave 26. Here, in the Final Renunciation, the Buddha leaves his mortal body to achieve divine bliss. Below him are grieving disciples, who mourn the passing of their Master. One of these grieving figures is shown in the detail (right). See also p. 47*

The façade of Cave 19 is profusely decorated with some of the finest sculptural friezes at Ajanta. Of these, the Buddhas flanking the entrance are most inspired. In the example seen here, the ornate crown which is held by flying ganas *above the head foreshadows the crowned Buddhas of the later period.*

undoubtedly rank among the finest and most inspired sculptures in the entire heritage of the Indian subcontinent.

DISCOVERY AND APPRECIATION

The first scholarly report on the Ajanta caves was by James Fergusson who read a paper at the Royal Asiatic Society of Great Britain and Ireland in 1843, in which he described these rock-cut 'temples'. Spurred by this report, extracts from which are reprinted as an Appendix (see pp. 242ff.), the British Government soon sponsored three major attempts to make reproductions of these paintings so that they could be brought to the attention of the world. On 6 April 1886 the *Times of India* expressed the view that 'In a national under-taking of this nature the Secretary of State should make it his special business to see that no pains and no money are spared for the initial outlay. The panels and decorative work alone will render the book [containing reproductions] indispensable to every important art school in Europe.'

Herculean efforts to reproduce the paintings were made by several artists: Major Robert Gill from 1844 to 1863, John Griffiths from 1872 to 1885 and James Burgess from 1877 to 1882. Gill's paintings were displayed at the Crystal Palace at Sydenham in 1866. Unfortunately, when the exhibition caught fire, most of his work was destroyed. Four sur-viving copies are presently in the Victoria and Albert Museum in London. Undaunted by this tragic loss, Gill returned to Ajanta and took up his labour of love again. However, his task was fated to remain unfulfilled, for he fell ill and died at Bhusawal, not very far from Ajanta, where his tomb can still be visited.

John Griffiths, Superintendent (later Principal) of the Sir Jamshedji Jijibhai School of Art, Bombay, along with many of his students, was the next to undertake the challenging task. Griffiths took to his work with great zeal, for he foresaw the impact of the Ajanta murals on the future of art in India. However, misfortune again struck when Griffiths' work was on display at the Indian Museum, South Kensington: many of his paintings were

One of the watercolour copies of scenes at Ajanta made by Lady Herringham and her helpers, published in 1915:
*the ritual bath (*abhishek*) scene from the Mahajanaka Jataka in Cave 1 (see pp. 98–9).*

damaged when fire broke out in the exhibition. The surviving ones, which were published in 1896, served to draw the attention of art historians more than ever before to the great importance of the Ajanta paintings in the context of world art. Unfortunately, however, Griffiths also unwittingly began the damage to the ancient paintings caused by human intervention. In order to brighten the details of certain paintings, he applied varnish to them. The disastrous effect of this was almost immediate. When Maurice Maindron visited Ajanta in 1884, he observed that 'the varnish had flaked off from all parts, carrying with it the painting, the fragments of which were accumulated on the ground.' (*L'Art indienne*, Paris, 1898).

In the meantime, James Fergusson and James Burgess of the Archaeological Survey of India carried out a systematic study of the paintings, architectural details, sculptures and inscriptions of the Ajanta caves. To the best of my knowledge, all that remains of the comprehensive reproductions of Burgess are black-and-white photographs which are now in the India Office Collection of the British Library in London.

From 1909 to 1911, Lady Herringham and her team of assistants again laboured long hours in the Ajanta caves and succeeded in producing a set of watercolour copies of some of the paintings which were published in a beautiful volume by the India Society in 1915. However, as she wrote, 'in reality, the technique of original work was so sure and perfect that none of us were good enough executants to repeat it.'

Lady Herringham's book and the work of those before her helped in bringing the paintings of Ajanta to the attention of the Western world. Over a century after the caves were rediscovered, the paintings were described in the *Burlington Magazine* as 'perhaps the greatest artistic wonder of Asia'. In 1923, the renowned ballerina Anna Pavlova performed an 'Ajanta Ballet' at Covent Garden in London, with choreography based on gestures of figures depicted in the caves. In the meanwhile, a breeze from Ajanta had reached the vibrant art centre of Calcutta, where it stirred an exciting renaissance of the Indian tradition of painting. When she visited Ajanta, Lady Herringham had taken with her three artists from Calcutta, all students of the famous Abanindranath Tagore: Nandalal Bose, Asit Haldar and Samarendra Gupta. For these painters, who up till then had not known of the existence of any beautiful paintings from India's past, this journey to Ajanta became a great pilgrimage. Their work of copying the murals on the walls became an act of homage to artist ancestors; for artists, who had never known that their own country had a rich tradition of painting, the revelation of Ajanta was exhilarating. They came back to Calcutta and shared the joy of their discovery and their excitement with colleagues. Soon there sprang up schools of a new art form inspired by the country's own rich tradition rediscovered at Ajanta. Since then, Ajanta has always retained a very special place in the imaginations and the minds of the Indian people. Its artistic legacy became and has remained a symbol of the great beauty of India's rich past and has also served as an immense source of inspiration for exploration in the fields of other Indian art forms.

THE ROLE OF PHOTOGRAPHY

In additon to the copies of the murals prepared by artists, numerous attempts at reproducing the Ajanta paintings by means of colour photography were also made. In the earlier part of the twentieth century, photography was not sufficiently advanced to capture the colours of the paintings accurately. In recent years, the Archaeological Survey of India has not permitted the use of photographic lights because of the risk of causing damage to the ancient paintings. Strictly limited attempts to photograph some of the panels with the aid of strong lights were allowed, but these too failed to produce accurate results.

The first known attempt to photograph the murals was carried out in 1911 by Victor Goloubew and the results were published in a book containing 59 monochrome prints in 1927. The Archaeological Department of the Government of the Nizam of Hyderabad took note of the progressive deterioration of the paintings and launched a major restoration and photographic initiative. The Italian restorers Cecconi and Orsini were engaged by the Nizam to work at Ajanta for two seasons in 1920–21 and 1921–22. They removed the crust of dust and dirt which had formed over the paintings, as well as coats of varnish which had earlier been indiscriminately applied. Thereafter, Mr E.L. Vassey was assigned to the task and spent five months at Ajanta photographing the paintings. Vassey's negatives formed the basis of a descriptive four-volume work, written by Ghulam Yazdani, which included 232 black-and-white illustrations and 88 colour plates.

Attempts to photograph the Ajanta paintings and present them in reproductions as faithful as possible to their true colours continued, and books featuring limited numbers of colour plates have been published from time to time over the past fifty years. An album of 33 reproductions (1 monochrome, 32 in colour) produced by Madanjeet Singh was published in 1954 by New York Graphic Society, by arrangement with UNESCO. Some years later, in 1965, his *Cave Paintings of Ajanta*, with additional text and line drawings, appeared. David L. De Harport spent six months in India in 1955 when, with the assistance of two photographers assigned by the Archaeological Survey of India (ASI), he photographed the Ajanta murals; the following year, twenty of Harport's transparencies were published in a joint venture by the ASI and the Lalit Kala Academy under the title *Ajanta Paintings*. A small UNESCO publication with 28 reproductions in colour was also prepared from this material and was published in 1963. Another book was published by the Archaeological Survey of India, edited by its Director-General, Dr A. Ghosh; this work, *Ajanta Murals*, which included 85 plates in colour, appeared in 1967. These plates are all close-ups of the figures in the paintings as, in the words of the editor, 'Circumstances at Ajanta do not make it possible to take photographs of large scenes . . . the colour on the surface, shiny with shellac under artificial light, reacts differently from place to place . . .'. Line drawings based on narrative scenes were also included, and a few examples have been reproduced here by courtesy of the ASI (see pp. 13, 32, 36, 38, 60–2). All in all, however, the exquisite and haunting beauty of these paintings seemed fated to remain confined to the dim interiors of the remote caves.

In 1990, while I was visiting the Department of Culture of the Government of India in New Delhi, it was brought to my attention for the first time that the world-famous paintings of the Ajanta caves had never been photographed comprehensively or in accurate colour. I was also informed that the true and luminous quality of the colours and the depth and richness of detail of the murals were not apparent to the eye even when one visited the site. The reason for this is that, in order to protect the ancient paintings, the Archaeological Survey of India have installed only dim lighting in the caves, which excludes much of the light at the upper end of the colour spectrum. Thus, the paintings are perceived to have a very orangish cast as compared to their real colours. The blues and greens in particular are largely lost in the viewing and the colour cast which is created takes away much of the sense of depth in the painting, as well as the luminosity of the colours themselves.

Photography in low light has long been a passion with me. It began with my enchantment with scenes at night, particularly when the moon was full. There is a certain sense of magic in the peace of the night which has drawn me repeatedly to monuments such as the churches of Old Goa. Here, amidst the deserted remains of a once-great metropolis, the gentle fingers of the moonlight do not disturb the dust of the centuries which lies upon the churches. It has also given me great pleasure to work in the serene and dimly lit interiors of churches and other houses of God. The most fascinating outcome of this approach is that the results have consistently proved far superior to pictures of the same subjects when photographed in the conventional manner with the use of strong lights. The luminosity of colour, particularly the glow of gold, and the depth and the three-dimensional quality of these pictures have constantly delighted viewers. Indeed, in the case of the Ajanta photographs which form the basis of the illustrations in this book, it has been a special pleasure to hear artists constantly comment that these pictures 'are like paintings, not photographs'.

On hearing about the yet unseen exquisite beauty of Ajanta, I was drawn immediately to take up the challenge of photographing these murals in complete detail and to capture the full richness of their colours in all their nuances and shades. Here was the greatest treasure of India's heritage of painting, permanently cloaked in the darkness of the caves. Truly this was the ultimate task for which the patient hours spent over many years of photographing in low ambient light conditions had prepared me. I applied to the Archaeological Survey of India for permission to photograph the paintings and this was granted since I did not intend to use lights which might damage the paintings. An official assignment to undertake the photography could not be obtained, however, as, not surprisingly, there were many among the authorities who thought that the project I was embarking on was an impossible one.

In 1991 and 1992, I made two separate visits to the Ajanta site. In the course of each visit the murals of the caves were documented in as exhaustive detail as possible. Having benefited greatly from the experience of the first visit and having come to know the paintings of Ajanta intimately through many viewings of the photographs, the results of the work undertaken during the second visit (which are reproduced here) proved to be fully satisfying. My colleague Sangitika Nigam accompanied me on both these visits. She researched the *Jataka* stories and carefully studied the details of the narrative scenes on the walls. A thorough and careful record of the entire photo-documentation on both occasions was also maintained by her.

When these colour transparencies were first shown in New Delhi, the Director-General of the Archaeological Survey of India remarked, 'You have really conquered the darkness.' His words made all the effort over the long hours in the dark caves, the care and all the painstaking work seem worthwhile. Subsequently, those who have loved Ajanta, scholars and curators of art the world over, have expressed their happiness at being able to distinguish the details and the many subtle nuances of the paintings which they had never been able to discern before. I am humbled by the abundance and warmth of their appreciation – reactions which I had not anticipated. The keen interest with which Ajanta has also been received by audiences at the universities and museums where these transparencies have been shown has given me a deep sense of fulfilment. The present book will, I hope, help to bring the exquisite work of these many noble but anonymous master painters to the hearts of lovers of art everywhere.

All the interior photographs were taken in conditions of available light. The principal colour plates are arranged in the order in which we approach the caves illustrated: nos. 1, 2, 16 and 17. General views of the gorge, façades of the caves and some examples of the fine sculpture have also been included so that the reader may have a good visual understanding of the majestic site. Plans of the principal painted caves featured have also been included (see pp. 234–7).

THE IMPACT OF AJANTA ON ASIAN ART

In his Introduction to *Ajanta* by Ghulam Yazdani, published in 1930, Laurence Binyon, a leading authority on Asian art, wrote:

> In the art of Asia what a supreme and central position Ajanta owns! . . . Whoever studies the art of China and Japan, at whatever time he begins, starts on a long road which will lead him ultimately to Ajanta.

Buddhism spread far and wide from India along the trade routes leading northwards through Tibet and Afghanistan to China, and from there to Korea, Japan and other countries. Buddhist artistic traditions travelled with the message of the Buddha. The paintings of the many caves at Tun-huang in China are directly reminiscent of Ajanta. Even the art of Japan is a flower at the end of a long branch which carries still the fragrance that reminds us of its roots at Ajanta. The Vajrapani and other Bodhisattavas that occur in Japanese paintings are the same gentle apostles from Ajanta, filtered through the imagination of another race and moulded by the hands of other artists. The artistic tradition was also carried along with the teachings of the Buddha to Sri Lanka and the countries of South-East Asia.

Ajanta is indeed an enchanted place, a remote site where one of the greatest traditions of the art of the world flowered, and spread its seeds all over Asia. The humble painters had a great vision, a vision of humanity and compassion that remains just as moving and enthralling today.

NOTE ON THE *JATAKA* STORIES
by Sangitika Nigam

A central feature of the philosophical traditions of India is the belief in the transmigration of the soul and the law of Karma, according to which we each decide our own fate. Our deeds in the present life determine the form of our next birth and the conditions of that life to come. Since all forms of life are considered to be interrelated and are all manifestations of the divine, the soul takes birth in the form of different animals as well as human beings.

In India there is a long tradition of recounting the tales of the previous lives of heroes and saints. Mythological and religious literature from time immemorial abounds with such stories. The Buddha himself told his followers many stories about his former births. These are interesting parables called *Jatakas*, which serve to depict the various qualities of virtuous living which the Master taught. Many of the stories draw freely upon the vast oral Brahmanical traditions as well as the rich folklore.

The inclusion of the *Jatakas* in the canonical Buddhist literature of the fourth century BC shows that these stories must always have been integral to the religious literature of the faith. The depiction of scenes from these 'birth-stories' in the reliefs of the early Buddhist shrines of Sanchi, Amravati and Bharhut also illustrate that they were widely known around the third century BC.

The ancient Pali work entitled *The Jataka* contains 537 such stories of the Buddha's previous lives. Besides illustrating Buddhist doctrines by appropriate examples, these stories are also of great value in presenting a vivid picture of the social life and customs of ancient India.

Each tale opens with a preface which recounts the particular circumstances in the Buddha's life which led him to tell 'the birth-story'. The story then reveals some event from the long series of his previous lives as a Bodhisattva, that is a being on his path of evolution towards the attainment of Buddhahood. Having told the story, the Buddha identifies the different persons in the *Jataka* in their present births at the time of his discourse. The *Jatakas* persuade us, through the exemplary and inspiring lives led by the Bodhisattva, to follow a life of virtue and compassion in this world.

Scenes from the Mahajanaka Jataka *painted in Cave 1 (see pp. 84ff): the depiction of the royal palace and its distractions precedes the king's decision to abandon the worldly life (see pp. 90–5) and become a* bhikshu *or mendicant. The ritual bath before the king sets out from the palace (see pp. 98–9) is seen below, together with the unrelated scene in which the severed heads of four young men are presented on a platter (see pp. 102–3).*

The walls of Ajanta are resplendent with the exquisite depictions of the *Jatakas* (an outline of each story precedes the relevant colour plates). The artists working at Ajanta were probably guided by Buddhist monks who had an intimate knowledge of the religious texts of their times. These parables, which had become very close to the hearts of the people, are painted here with a humanity and vividness which has never been surpassed.

In reproducing individual scenes from narrative paintings it is not always possible to convey in words the relationship of one to another, whether placed above or below, to the left or the right. A small selection of line drawings has therefore been included to help the reader in visualizing the artists' treatment of a few of the *Jataka* stories as illustrated in the colour plates.

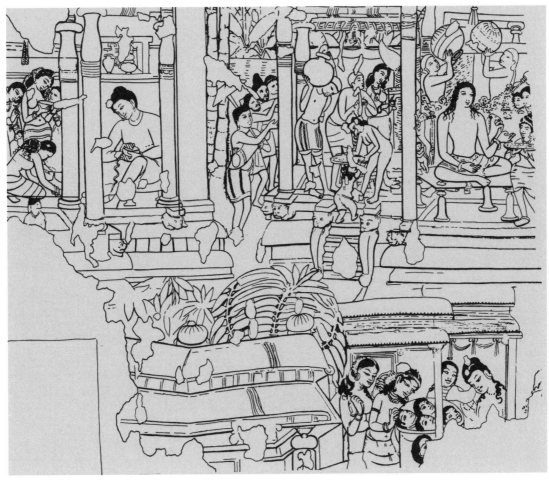

ABOVE: *Part of the* Vidhurapandita Jataka *painted in Cave 2 (see p. 130). Here Princess Irandati is shown on a swing in the garden, and, on the right, members of the royal Naga family are seen in conversation (p. 131).*

BELOW: *Part of the* Visvantara Jataka *painted in Cave 17 (see pp. 160–3). The action moves from right to left, where the princely couple are shown departing from the palace through the garden.*

Cave 1

Cave 2

Cave 16

Cave 17

Cave 1

At the beginning of the horseshoe bend on the north side of the Ajanta site is the most magnificently painted *vihara* in India. Although there are no inscriptions in this cave to establish its date, on stylistic grounds it appears to be a little earlier than Cave 2, has inscriptions dating from the first half of the sixth century.

In this *vihara* the visitor is transported into a world of loveliness, in which the painter has achieved the highest standards of beauty in terms of both line and colour. Indeed, in this cave every painting conveys a sense of the painter's devotion to his task.

The cave formerly had a portico, but this collapsed before the Ajanta site was rediscovered in 1819. The plan of the *vihara* comprises a verandah, a large hall and a shrine beyond. The verandah, which is 64 ft (19.50 m) long, 9 ft 3 in. (2.82 m) wide and 13 ft 6 in. (4.11 m) high, has a cell at either end. A door in the centre leads into the grand hall, which is 64 ft (19.50 m) square. There are twenty pillars in all, leaving aisles about 9 ft 6 in. (2.90 m) wide on all four sides. For a plan of this cave see p. 234.

For a plan of this cave see p. 234.

The façade of Cave 1, which dates from the sixth century. This is the most magnificent example of a vihara (monastery) among all the rock-hewn temples of India. Originally, this cave had a porch which has collapsed. Above the pillars are several bands of skilfully carved reliefs depicting scenes from the life of the Buddha, as well as portrayals of contemporary life.

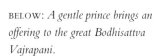

BELOW: *A gentle prince brings an offering to the great Bodhisattva Vajrapani.*

RIGHT: *The Majesty of the Spirit is revealed through the divine aspect of the Bodhisattva Vajrapani, the Bearer of the Thunderbolt. This regal being, on the right of the entrance to the antechamber of the main shrine of Cave 1, is one of the most exalted masterpieces of Ajanta's art. The glorious workmanship of the jewelled crown is truly remarkable. In the centre of the crown is a damaged figure which, though not identifiable in its present state, is of immense significance in the study of Buddhist iconography. This is the earliest known depiction of a figure wearing the head-dress of a Bodhisattva. In later Buddhist art such figures in the crown indicate the association of the Bodhisattva with one of the Dhyani Buddhas, each representing a different aspect of the Buddha's wisdom; they are seen in all the Mahayana Buddhist countries of Asia.*

Below the Bodhisattva is a dark
princess to whom a lady is shown
offering lotuses. This leads us to
assume that the princess is the consort
of the Bodhisattva Vajrapani. Her
features are very refined and the
delineation of the eyes, with hazel-
brown irises, is extremely realistic.
Although the painting has suffered
considerable damage, it is still regarded
as one of the finest works of Indian
artistic genius and counts among the
most outstanding portraits of feminine
beauty made in any part of the world.

To the left of the entrance to the antechamber of the main shrine is seen the gentle figure of the Bodhisattva Padmapani, the Bearer of the Lotus (opposite). This benign apostle is painted amidst the many activities of the teeming world around him; closer views are seen in the details illustrated overleaf. Next to the Bodhisattva Padmapani is painted a dark princess (above) holding a lotus – an indication that she is his consort. Her face has a very serene expression and the treatment of her limbs is exquisite. This portrait is, indeed, one of the most graceful paintings of Ajanta.

Monkeys, which are seen playing above the left shoulder of the Padmapani, represent the distractions of everyday worldly activity.

OPPOSITE ABOVE: *A* kinnara, *a celestial musician who is part-bird and part-human, is painted above the Padmapani on his right. Again, his divine music is symbolic of the pleasant pastimes which may serve as distractions to One who is on the Path of True Knowledge. The stringed musical instrument, complete with tuning knobs, on which the* kinnara *plays is of particular interest as it adds to our knowledge of the culture of the painter's times.*

OPPOSITE BELOW: *In the panel of the Padmapani, a delightful detail of peacocks painted with lapis lazuli to convey the iridescent blue of their neck plumage.*

Sibi Jataka

King Sibi was a previous birth of Lord Buddha: the Bodhisattva on his way to Enlightenment. In this *Jataka* the Lord Indra (who figures often in Buddhist lore as *Sakka*) puts to the test his qualities of righteousness and justice (see also pp. 226–7).

Pursued by a hawk, a frightened pigeon came to King Sibi who took him under his protection and saved him from the predator. However, the hawk also appealed to the king for justice. He said that he needed fresh meat for his nourishment and the pigeon was its legitimate prey. Thus, the just and kind King Sibi found himself in a dilemma. The only solution for him, which was acceptable to the hawk, was that the king cut off some of his own flesh, equal in weight to the pigeon, and give it to the hawk.

The hawk and the pigeon were, in fact, the disguised Lords Indra and Agni respectively. As Agni in the form of the pigeon was placed on the scales, he made himself heavier and heavier, causing the king to cut off larger parts of his own flesh. Finally King Sibi had to climb bodily onto the scales.

When the Gods saw that the king was willing to make the supreme sacrifice, they revealed themselves in their true forms. King Sibi's wounds were healed and praise was showered upon him in recognition of his virtues.

The Sibi Jataka *is seen on the inside of the front wall to the left of the doorway as one enters Cave 1. The story also occurs in the Hindu and Jain traditions.*

LEFT: *The just and noble Bodhisattva King Sibi stands next to the weighing scales. The gentle expression on his face is poignant as he prepares to sacrifice his own self to uphold the quality of justice.*

BELOW: *A prince and princess in a pavilion in the palace look compassionately towards King Sibi.*

OVERLEAF: *A* kirtimukha *carved on a pillar. The caves are profusely ornamented with carvings of mythical creatures like this one, as well as other motifs such as makaras, lotus-creepers, pearl-hangings and jewel-like patterns. They help to create a warm and rich atmosphere in the cave.*

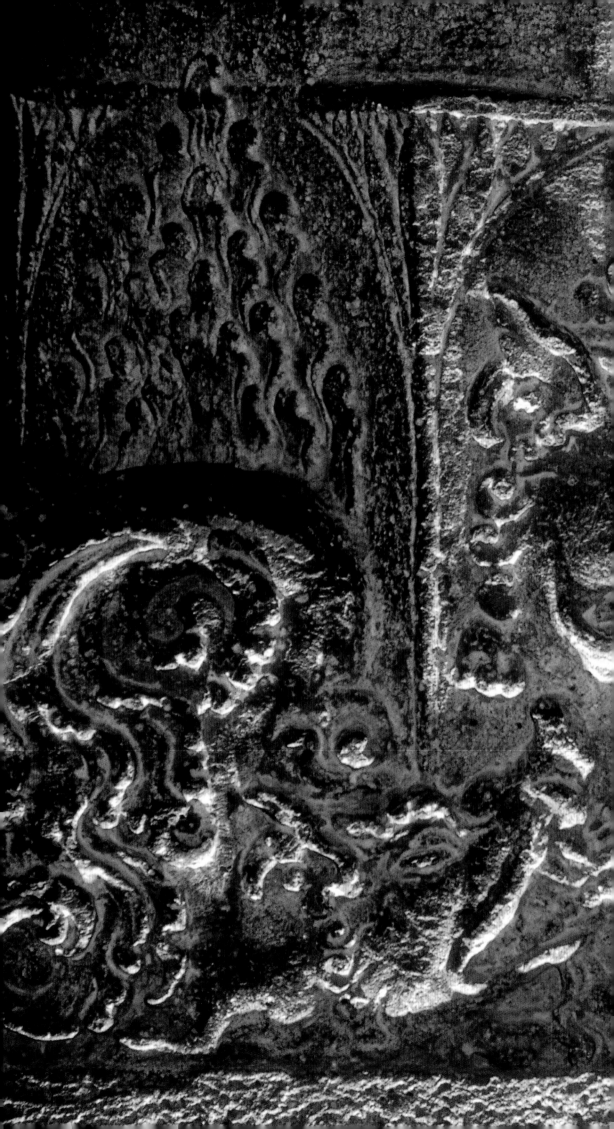

The Conversion of Nanda

Nanda was a cousin of the Buddha. Among the incidents of the Lord's life, his conversion of Nanda is one of the favourite themes of Buddhist artists. The story is painted to the right of the Sibi Jataka on the front left wall of Cave 1 (we find another very sensitive depiction of it in Cave 16 – see pp. 150–1). In this detail (right) we see Nanda after he has renounced his palace life to become a wandering mendicant (bhikshu). This gentle soul, who is made so graceful by his divine introspection, is seen here begging for alms at his own palace door. This detail is one of the most soulful masterpieces of Ajanta's art. Nanda with his inward look radiates a serene peacefulness which holds the attention of the viewer most compellingly.

Nanda's wife Queen Janapada-kalyani (left) has been informed that her husband, once the king, has come to the palace door begging for alms. The queen is deeply disturbed by these unusual events and wonders how to win back the attention of her husband. Interestingly, this is the only panel at Ajanta in which the women are seen wearing the traditional Indian bindi (an auspicious circular symbol of marriage) on the forehead.

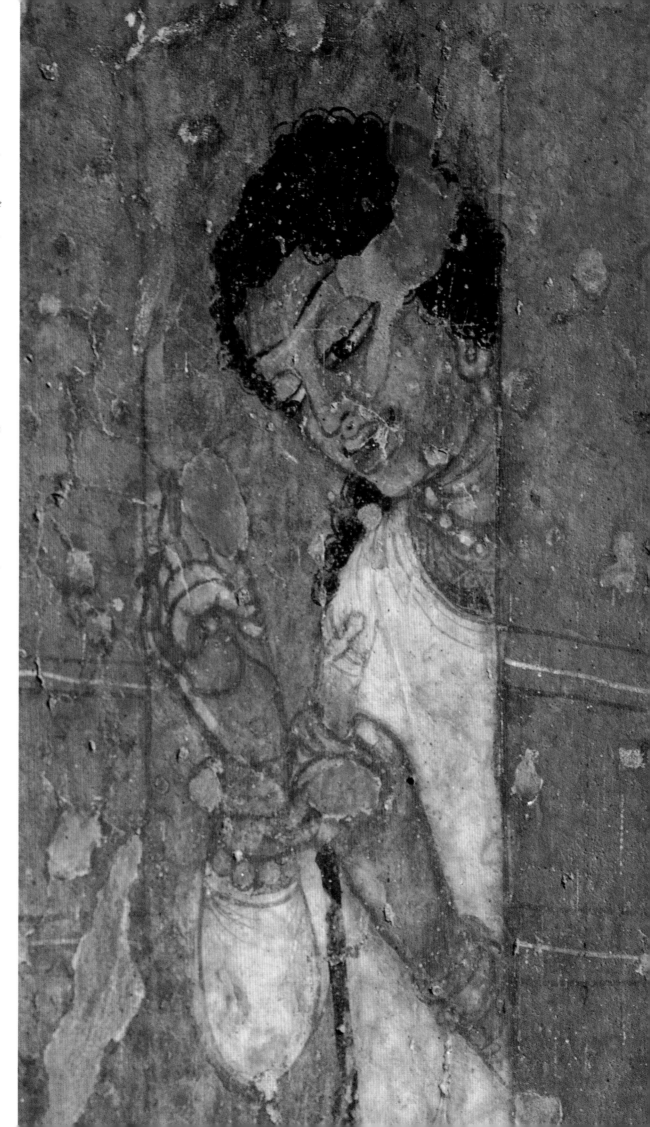

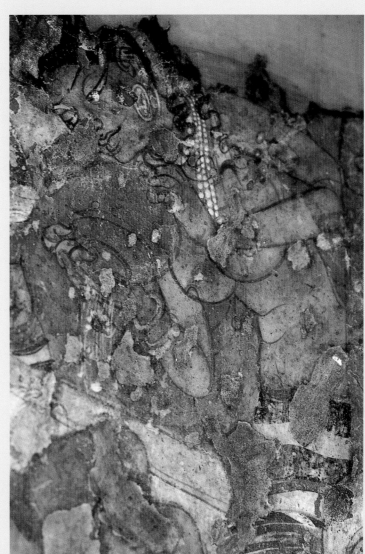

OPPOSITE: *An agitated palace attendant is portrayed in the story of King Nanda. One can well imagine the confusion and the rush of mixed emotions created within the palace by the appearance of the king in his new state as a mendicant.*

In two other details from the story, palace maids are seen pouring water over the lissom Queen Janapada- *kalyani as she pines for her husband (right), and taking an offering of food for the* bhikshu *at the palace door (below).*

Again the bindi *is seen on the maid's forehead and she also has a most unusual coiffure. Indeed, almost every conceivable hairstyle seems to have been prevalent in the days when the Ajanta caves were painted.*

Sankhapala Jataka

In the upper left portion of this panel, the King of Magadha (now an ascetic) is imparting the Law of Dharma to Sankhapala the Naga king. The figure of the ascetic has suffered considerable damage, but that of Sankhapala is better preserved. He is shown with his hands folded in devotion and humility.

A charming detail is a woman who is seated on the ground with her back to the viewer, also listening to the sermon. Her pose shows great observation and skill: she is squatting on the ground with crossed legs, leaning on her left hand which is placed on the ground, while her right hand with the elbow resting on her knee supports her head in a very realistic manner.

To her right is a dwarf, who brings an offering of flowers for the ascetic. The religious austerity of the scene is offset by the somewhat comic effect of his long trunk and wild expression.

Once the Bodhisattva was born as Duyyodhana, the son of the King of Magadha. When the prince came of age, his father handed over the reins of the kingdom to him and retired to live the life of an ascetic.

One day when he visited his father's hermitage, Duyyodhana saw the splendour and wealth of a Naga king who had come with his retinue to hear the ascetic's discourse. Being struck by the Naga king's grandeur, the Bodhisattva wished that he be reborn in such a form. The Boddhisattva's wish was granted and he was born as Sankhapala, King of the Nagas. After some time of dwelling in the luxuries and pleasures of the serpent world, he realized the futility of worldly prosperity and decided to end his meaningless life. Accordingly, he went and lay on an ant-hill.

The Serpent King was spotted by a band of hunters, who captured him and treated him cruelly. This was seen by a merchant named Alara, who was moved by pity for the serpent and had him released by offering cattle and gold coins to the hunters. Out of gratitude, the Bodhisattva King Sankhapala invited Alara to the Naga world. For a year Alara revelled in its luxuries and heavenly delights, but was finally influenced by the wisdom of the Bodhisattva. He then gave up the glory and pleasures of the serpent world and went to the Himalayas to become an ascetic and to preach the Law. In Alara's words from the *Jataka*:

'Men fall like fruit, to perish straight away,

All bodies, young and old alike, decay:

In holy orders only find I rest,

The true and universal is the best.'

(translated by H.T. Francis; edited by E.B. Cowell)

The Serpent King is dragged along by hunters who have put a rope through its nose (left). The effort in pulling on the rope has been most dynamically depicted. Behind the hunters is a man watching with sympathy as the cruelty is inflicted upon the serpent. Below the serpent, Alara offers coins and his oxen to the hunters to induce them to release the serpent. The various attitudes of the cattle show the painter's acute observation and knowledge of animal life.

Painted to the left of the previous scene is an elegant princess (below, right), drawn with long and sinuous lines. She stands behind the Naga king, listening with close attention to the sermon.

In the bottom left of the mural we see the Naga King Sankhapala with his rescuer Alara (below, left). The features of the Bodhisattva Sankhapala are extremely graceful and show a remarkable contrast to the coarse features of the merchant Alara.

The practice of worshipping Naga or Serpent kings is one of great antiquity, and they were adopted in the beliefs prevalent at various times in India's early history. In Buddhist thought they are regarded as evolved beings on the True Path to enlightenment, their original fierce nature having been tempered by the compassion of the Buddha's message.

83

Mahajanaka Jataka

Mahajanaka was the son of Aritthajanaka, who had been banished from the Kingdom of Mithila by his brother Polajanaka. Mahajanaka became a merchant in order to amass a large enough fortune to enable him to reconquer the kingdom which had been usurped by his uncle.

After many adventures, including a shipwreck, he returned to the Kingdom of Mithila. In the meantime, King Polajanaka had died leaving no son to succeed him on the throne. He had only one daughter, the wise and learned Sivali. On his deathbed, the king had expressed the wish that she should be married only to a man who could fulfil three conditions: he should know the head end of a square bed; draw out the sixteen treasures which were hidden in his kingdom; and be able to string a bow which required the strength of a thousand men. Mahajanaka fulfilled all three requirements, married the beautiful Sivali, and so became the King of Mithila.

However, the pomp and luxuries of royal life soon lost their attraction for the Bodhisattva and he decided to renounce his kingdom to become an ascetic. Queen Sivali was heartbroken and made many unsuccessful attempts to distract him and persuade him not to give up the kingdom. Ultimately she followed him into the forest and, realizing that he could not proceed further on his Path unless he was able to dissuade her from following him, he broke a stalk of *munja* grass and said to her, 'See, Sivali this stalk cannot be joined again. So like to a *munja* reed full grown, live on, O Sivali, alone.' Sivali realized the fateful meaning of his words. She fell into a faint and as she lay overcome with grief, the Bodhisattva proceeded on his journey to the Himalayas. There he meditated upon the Truth, never to return to the worldly life.

*A scene from the Mahajanaka Jataka.
This story of the Bodhisattva is
magnificently painted over most of the
left wall of Cave 1, and extends onto
part of the rear wall of the cave. Here,
in the upper part of the panel, an
ascetic is shown delivering a sermon.
Among those listening is King
Mahajanaka, seen with his hands
folded in reverence. See also pp. 92–3.*

Details from the sermon scene shown on p. 85.

RIGHT: *The great ascetic imparting to King Mahajanaka the knowledge of the True Path of Renunciation.*

BELOW: *A delightful detail, in which antelope are also listening with rapt attention to the discourse: at Ajanta there are no barriers between the world of the animals and that of mankind. We are reminded here that Lord Buddha himself had been born previously in the form of several different animals. Hence, the artist depicts a faith which has a profound belief in the unity of all forms of life.*

The Bodhisattva listening with devotion to the ascetic's words. Mahajanaka was a great and glorious king who had, in fact, won back the lands that had earlier been lost by his father. Yet here we find this powerful ruler with hands folded, gazing with adoration towards the simple ascetic. It is this quality of humility which enriches the Life of the Spirit.

King Mahajanaka, having heard the wise words of the sage and returned to the palace, decides to renounce the worldly life. In this detail he is shown announcing his decision in the palace; behind him is his mother, who appears worried by her son's resolve.

RIGHT: *Before the king as he makes his decision known is his beautiful wife Queen Sivali, who is perplexed by her husband's desire to leave the palace and part from her. The lower garments worn by the women are woven in the form of* ikhat, *which is still practised in India. The fabrics of the upper garments are silks and muslins, so fine that they appear diaphanous.*

The artists' minute attention to detail in these paintings is extraordinary. The gentle curve of the strings of pearls hanging beneath the queen's bosom depicts a lightly swinging movement with exquisite realism. The curls of hair upon her neck and shoulders emphasize her vulnerability at this moment when her husband has chosen to leave her.

LEFT: *Three of the palace maids, painted behind the queen, respond with shock and sadness to the most unexpected news that the king intends to renounce his worldly life and leave their mistress the queen.*

Amazement is writ large upon the face of one maid and we see the sorrowful glances of the other two. The directness of the warm human touch in this moment of grief is clearly evident as they empathize with the queen's deep sense of impending loss.

A palace scene from the Mahajanaka Jataka: the king and queen are shown seated in a pavilion watching a dance performance arranged by Queen Sivali. Four details from this scene are shown on the following pages.

OPPOSITE ABOVE: *Seated next to the king in the royal pavilion is Queen Sivali, looking tenderly towards him. Another woman stands behind the queen, delicately holding a conch in her hand.*

OPPOSITE BELOW: *A most unusual and realistic moment captured by the vivid imagination of the painters of Ajanta: a maid is shown pressing the legs of the queen, but obviously she is distracted by the dancer behind her and, even as she touches the queen's legs, she turns to look in that direction.*

RIGHT: *Between the pavilions of the royal couple and the dancer are two other palace maids. One is in a pensive mood and the other leans upon her shoulder, looking at her, as if questioning. The realism and inexhaustible variety of feelings and expressions of the figures are a source of constant wonder. Each of the countless individuals depicted in these Jatakas has a unique and distinctive expression. The lower garment of the pensive maid has colourful stripes and beautiful decorations.*

A gorgeously attired dancer and musicians, who have been summoned by Queen Sivali to distract the king from his resolve. This scene is a unique instance in Indian art where a complete orchestra and dancer are all women. There are seven musicians: two flautists, two playing cymbals, one a pair of drums (dhol), another playing a double drum called a mridang, and one playing a stringed instrument. All these musical instruments, practically unchanged, remain in use in India.

The painting closely follows the directions laid down in the ancient Indian treatise of painting, the Chitrasutra of the Vishnudharmottra. According to the text, dancers should be shown most exquisitely attired, as we see here. She is bedecked with a large variety of ornaments, including an arsi (thumb-ring with a miniature mirror), ear-rings with most elaborate designs and ornaments of the head, comprising gold or pearl strings. The coiffure is very pleasing and depicts strings of flowers intertwined with the hair in her chignon.

In keeping with the directions of the Chitrasutra, her scarves are also seen swirling behind her with her movements. The pose caught of the dancer is most interesting. It is typical of Indian dance movements still in use today, and serves to show that these traditions were already well established more than 1,500 years ago

95

ABOVE: *King Mahajanaka, not distracted by all the diversions of the palace, goes ahead with his resolve. Here we see him riding out of the palace gates, leaving worldly affairs behind him.*

OPPOSITE: *Behind the head of King Mahajanaka's horse is a man wearing a most interesting block-printed shawl with a duck pattern. Also seen here is another man wearing a diaphanous cloth with a clearly discernible design.*

Another scene from the Mahajanaka Jataka, *painted on the back wall of Cave 1 to the left of the main shrine. Here we see the* abhishek *(ritual bath) of the king, which is to cleanse him before he dons the saffron robe signifying his final renunciation of the world.*

The profusely decorated palace pavilion with its bejewelled pillars speaks of a highly developed and prosperous civilization which must have existed when the cave was painted. Of particular interest is the straight-backed seat of the king, gorgeously carved with animal figures.

The feeling of the painting is very realistic. The moment is depicted in great detail, showing Mahajanaka's wet hair, a dwarf coming up the steps and handing over a tray to an adolescent girl, bearers bringing vessels of water; a graceful female attendant and others who are gathered in a group; and several mendicants who have come to beg for alms on this auspicious occasion.

In this complex panel we discern the careful arrangement of the composition in keeping with the closely linked traditions of painting and theatre. (These are set out in detail in the Vishnudharmottra, *as well as in the older text on drama and dance called the* Natyahastra *of* Bharata.) *The artist is so skilled and inspired that he has succeeded in presenting a large group of persons, each imbued with individual personality and feeling, while simultaneously – by the direction of their attention and actions – leading the viewer's eye to the central figure of Mahajanaka.*

RIGHT: *In this detail from the* Mahajanaka Jataka *women are shown bearing offerings for the king, who has now become a* bhikshu. *The flowing S-curve (frequently seen in Indian art) is beautifully delineated, from the reverential bending of the neck to the curve of the devotee's hip.*

In another detail (below) the bhikshu *is shown seated inside the pavilion, begging bowl in hand.*

LEFT: *A detail from the* abhishek *scene showing two attendants. The male attendant is most interestingly attired in what appears to be a tight shirt-like garment and wears a cap on his head. The dusky female attendant is invested with tenderness and feminine grace.*

On the back wall of the cave, below the
Mahajanaka Jataka, *is a very curious
unidentified scene. It appears as if the heads of
four young men are brought on a platter before
an ascetic who is seated in a palace pavilion,
rosary in hand.*

BELOW: *One of the heads from the
unidentified group.*

Campeya Jataka

The Bodhisattva was once born into a poor family. He used to go to a nearby river called Campa, where lived the magnificent Serpent King Campeya. Impressed by Campeya's glory, the Bodhisattva wished that he be reborn as a Naga king.

In his next life his wish came true, but as the years passed he became unhappy and discontented with his luxurious existence as the Serpent King. He tried to kill himself but his wife Sumana helped to rekindle his interest in life and with her beautiful companions succeeded in keeping him amused.

The Bodhisattva soon perceived that he would not be able to release himself from his sensual attachments if he continued to live in the Naga world. Thus he came out to lead a life of austerity in the world of men.

As Campeya lay on an ant-hill, a young Brahmin from Benaras saw the magnificent snake and captured him. The Brahmin then took him to the city and forced the serpent to dance. Soon his fame as a dancing snake spread throughout the kingdom and he was taken to the court of King Uggasena to perform before

him. The king and his people were enthralled by his dance and showered him with jewels.

In the meantime, Campeya's wife Sumana grew concerned about the fate of her husband and, on making enquiries about his whereabouts, appeared in King Uggasena's court. She pleaded with the king for the release of her husband. The king was touched by Sumana's devotion and offered great wealth to the Brahmin in exchange for the freedom of the snake. The Brahmin was ashamed of himself and, refusing the wealth offered to him, immediately released Campeya.

The Serpent King Campeya and Sumana then transformed themselves into a young man and a beautiful woman and thanked the king profusely for his kindness. They took the king with them to share the opulent luxuries of the Naga kingdom. The king then came to realize that the snake was none other than the Serpent King Campeya. At the end of seven days of the wondrous pleasures of the Naga world, he returned to his own kingdom at Benaras laden with wealth bestowed on him by the Serpent King. According to the *Jataka*, from that time on the ground was golden throughout India.

To the right of the Bodhisattva Vajrapani panel on the back wall of the cave is painted the Campeya Jataka. Here the Naga King Campeya is seen in his palace, very dejected as is obvious from his pose. Having enjoyed the pleasures of royal life and violated the rules of virtue, the Bodhisattva now deeply regrets his conduct.

The second scene of the jataka shows King Uggasena watching the performance of the snake, for which many people are gathered. On the right we see the snake-charmer seated on the ground. On the left is Sumana, the favourite consort of Campeya, who has brought her child with her.

Below the king is the most fascinating detail of this panel, with two men shown seated on the ground. The features of one of them, including the moustache and the tuft of hair on the back of his head, are still typical of the people of Benaras. His floral, silken angrakha *(upper garment) is* also reminiscent of the attire and the continuing textile industry of the city. The features, the hair style and the manner in which the other man wears his dhoti remain typical of the people of Orissa.

In a palace hall depicted in the third scene, Bodhisattva Campeya is seen in the teaching mudra, *showing King Uggasena the Righteous Path. The palace attendants and courtiers who crowd around to listen are depicted with consummate grace and skill.*

An amusing detail in the extreme right of the palace scene shows a maid carrying a platter of delicacies with flowers arranged around them. She listens to the sermon with rapt attention and is oblivious of the man behind her who quietly picks up one of the items on her platter. The curling locks of hair of the young maid are most charmingly portrayed.

ABOVE: *A Bacchanalian scene, painted on the ceiling, representing foreigners from the north-west of India. Buddhism had spread beyond the frontiers of India well before the Christian Era, and the artists active at Ajanta during the second creative phase were already quie accustomed to the presence of such visitors.*

RIGHT: *A detail from another damaged and unidentified scene, painted on the right-hand wall. It is significant, however, for it presents a different style of painting and the persons depicted appear, from their features and ornamentation, to belong to another race or country. Because Ajanta lay on the arterial trade route, it was open to influences from far and wide, and one may surmise that this is a representation of a wealthy merchant and his retinue from a foreign land.*

OVERLEAF : *The ceiling is painted with rich and exquisite detail. The themes of the ceiling paintings are quite different from the religious content of the murals. Here the painter gives free rein to his imagination and decorative skills. The flora and fauna of the times are depicted here, as well as legendary and mythical creatures.*

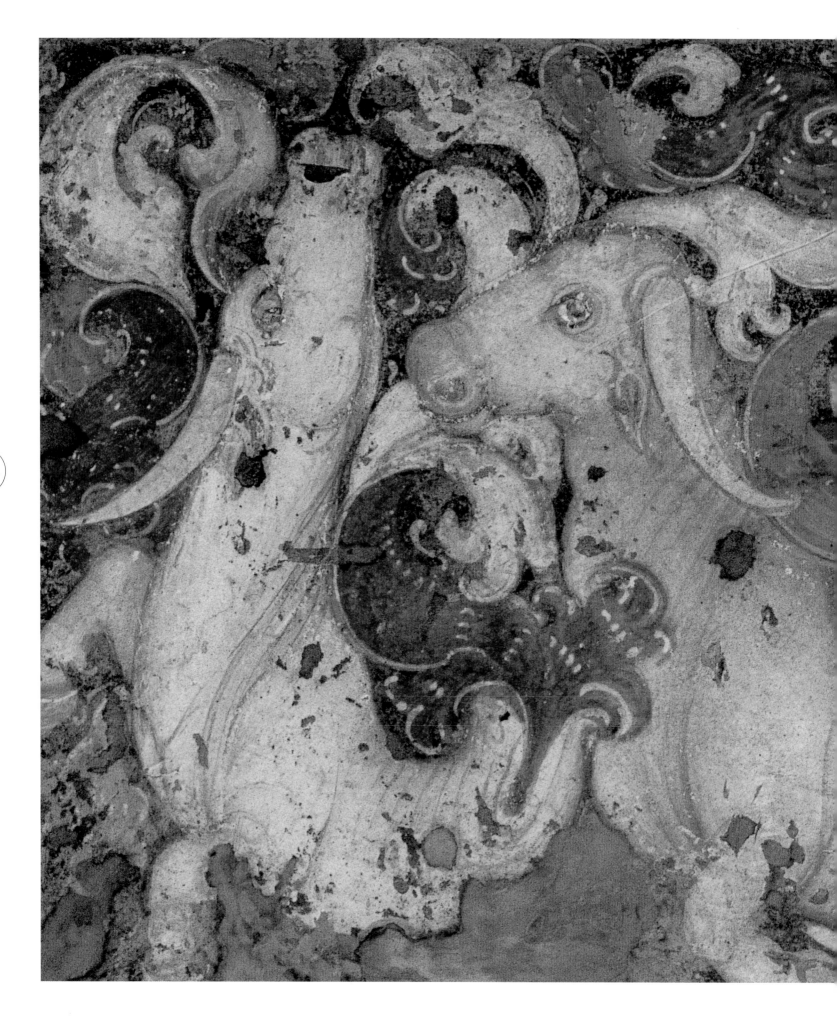

LEFT: *Individual panels from the ceiling: (top) a decorative vegetable motif; (centre) a most ingenious depiction of a creature that is a bull in front and gradually transformed into the gracefully curving lines which blend into the flora of the background (truly an expression of the oneness of all creatures) and (bottom) a comic scene with two gnomes at play.*

This beautifully observed light-footed elephant painted in one of the ceiling panels has been chosen as the official logo of the Government of India's Department of Tourism.

Like Cave 1, this is another beautifully painted *vihara*. It has numerous inscriptions which, on the basis of comparison with rock-cut writings elsewhere, belong to the first half of the sixth century. The inscriptions include beautiful verses such as the following:

'Blossoms are the ornaments of trees, it is flashes of lightning that adorn the big rain clouds, the lakes are adorned by lotuses and waterlilies with their intoxicated bees: but virtues brought to perfection are the proper ornaments of living beings.'

(translation by Kern, *Harvard Oriental Series*, vol. I).

This *vihara* is similar to that of Cave 1 in plan, but it is smaller in area (see p. 235). The verandah in front is 46 ft 3 in. (14.10 m) long and 7 ft 9 in. (2.36 m) wide. It has a chapel on each end, with beautifully carved façades. The main hall is 48 ft 4 in. x 47 ft 7 in. (14.73 x 14.50 m) and it has twelve elaborately carved pillars. There are ten cells intended as residences for *bhikshus* which

are placed around all four sides of the cave. The shrine in the centre of the back wall of the cave measures 14 x 11 ft (4.27 x 3.35 m) and on either side of it are subsidiary pillared chapels which have large sculpted figures. The chapel on the right depicts Panchika, the Lord of Wealth, and Hariti, the Divine Protectress of Children. The chapel on the left has two Yaksha figures, executed with considerable feeling and featuring detailed ornamentation.

All the walls of the cave and its ceiling were originally exquisitely painted. As is the case in the other caves, many of the paintings have been lost due to the ravages of time. Fortunately, however, there is also a considerable body of surviving paintings here, though they have become visibly darkened by the coats of shellac that were applied in the past. The details have therefore been obscured in many places, and the beauty of many of the figures can only be appreciated with close attention. The yellow cast of the shellac is also present almost everywhere in this cave.

In the chapel set on the right-hand side of the back wall are statues of Hariti and her consort Panchika, the Lord of Wealth. Hariti was a female demon who was in the habit of devouring children until the Buddha converted her to following the path of the Dharma.

Cave 2

A representation of the Miracle of Shravasti, painted on the right-hand wall of the antechamber of the main shrine. In order to silence the sceptics who did not believe the word of the Buddha, he manifested himself miraculously before them in a thousand different forms.

This painting, as well as other representations of the miracle in this cave, are clearly of a later date than the rest of the murals and, in their conventional repetition of the figure of the Buddha, they show a waning of the inspiration that was evident in the works of the earlier artists.

ABOVE: *Before his birth as the Buddha, the Bodhisattva, depicted here, dwelt in the Tushita Heaven. In the upper portion of the left wall of the cave, he is shown surrounded by other deities as he makes his decision to descend to Earth and to be born to Queen Mahamaya.*

Detail of the Bodhisattva in the Tushita Heaven. The mudra of his hands shows him to be in the Teaching attitude. Compared to most of the other paintings, the treatment here appears conventional and betrays a comparative lack of creative effort. This may be because the artist's mind was fully engaged with the religious character of the theme. The pose, with the subject directly facing the viewer and without the least inclination of the body, is extremely rare among the figures depicted at Ajanta.

On the left-hand wall of Cave 2 is the panel depicting the miraculous birth of the Buddha. Queen Mahamaya had a dream in which a white elephant went around her couch three times, struck her on the right side and entered her womb.

LEFT: *In this section of the painting the Queen with her husband King Suddhodana is shown telling the court astrologer Asita about her dream. Asita says that the dream signifies that the Queen will have a male child, who will either become Ruler of the World or will renounce his courtly life to become a great ascetic who will show the Righteous Path to the people.*

LEFT: *The Queen is worried and disturbed by the possibility that her child might become an ascetic. Here we see her deep in thought, leaning against a pillar. Asita, the astrologer, is before her and a female attendant gazes at her with great compassion in her eyes. The depiction of the slender and profusely bejewelled queen, resting upon the pillar behind her, is uniquely graceful. The lines of the figure, from her slightly bent head to the poetically slim waist, swelling into her generous hips, make this one of the most charming paintings of Ajanta.*

OPPOSITE: *After having carried the future Buddha in her womb for ten months, Queen Mahanaya gave birth while standing under a* sal *tree. She is depicted at this moment, holding a branch of the tree above her head. According to the traditional account of the birth of Gautama (the Buddha) in 567 BC, the infant Buddha emerged from his mother's right side.*

On the rear wall of Cave 2 are rows of seated Buddha figures in different postures. Unlike the repetitive and conventional depictions elsewhere (see pp. 118–19), these are lively and expressive portrayals. The figures are seated on lotuses, and it is most interesting to note the variety of designs on the bolsters behind them.

In the same chapel, amongst a group of playful children, a child is shown carrying a hen.

OPPOSITE: *Devotees bringing offerings. This is a painting on the left-hand wall of a chapel to the right of the shrine of the cave. The mural has been greatly appreciated by European visitors who detected in these figures a likeness to the early Madonnas of Christian art. Indeed, among the many styles of the different artists of Ajanta, the one seen in this chapel is among the most developed. The head-dresses of two of these figures are quite different from those depicted in other paintings here.*

Vidhurapandita Jataka

A story of wisdom and self-sacrifice

In the city of Indraprastha, ruled by King Dhananjaya, there was a wise minister named Vidhurapandita who was universally admired for his knowledge and abilities. One day, the Naga King Varuna was so impressed by his discourse that he presented the minister with a jewelled necklace of immense value. On hearing of this, his consort Queen Vimala was furious. She feigned illness and told her husband that she would die unless Vidhurapandita's heart was brought to her.

The perplexed Varuna took his beautiful daughter Irandati into his confidence and entreated her to seek a brave husband who could satisfy her mother's desire. Irandati agreed and was able to attract the powerful Yaksha general Purnaka. The Yaksha was riding past in the sky on his flying horse when he heard the sweet song of the maiden and fell in love with her. Irandati then persuaded him to agree to kill Vidhurapandita and bring back his heart.

The wily Purnaka knew of King Dhananjaya's weakness for the game of dice. By enticing him with a magnificent jewel endowed with magical qualities, he lured the king into a game of dice, with his minister Vidhurapandita as the stake. Purnaka won the game and began his journey back with the minister. On the way he tried many times to kill Vidhurapandita, but was unsuccessful. The good minister, who was in fact the Bodhisattva, then told Purnaka how to kill him and remove his heart.

Purnaka was struck by his display of courage and sacrifice and brought him back alive to the Naga court. Here, King Varuna and Queen Vimala were greatly enchanted by Vidhurapandita's wise discourses. After great and joyous celebrations, the Bodhisattva was allowed to return to Indraprastha.

This Jataka is painted in several episodes on the right-hand wall of Cave 2. As in the other paintings of Ajanta, the narrative scenes do not follow any formal sequence; the chronological movement may be from left to right, from right to left, or in any other arrangement which the artist chooses. Since the Jataka stories would have been well known to most viewers, this random placement would not have posed any practical problems for the communication of the story.

In the upper left section of this part of the right-hand wall of the cave, we see the episode of the game of dice played by Purnaka and King Dhananjaya, as well as the earlier event when the king is lured into the game.

In the right-hand section above, is a scene set in the Naga kingdom, where the royal family is shown listening with reverence to the discourse of the

Bodhisattva Vidhurapandita who has been brought there by Purnaka.

At the bottom left the setting is the court of Indraprastha, where King Dhananjaya has just lost his wager and is seen in discussion with Vidhurapandita. In the scene to the right, Vidhurapandita is shown delivering a farewell discourse to the ladies of the palace of Indraprastha.

BELOW: *According to the Jataka, in order to attract Purnaka, Irandati 'gathered all the flowers in the Himalayas … spread them upon a couch … and sang a sweet song'. Here, the painter has taken the liberty of placing her on a swing instead of a couch, so adding considerably to the liveliness of the scene. There is a delightful feeling of movement suggested by the curves of the ropes and by Irandati's pose, with her legs stretched out fully and her feet pressed together.*

The painting is in the tradition of Indian literature, in which the swing is constantly associated with romantic and poetic moments.

BELOW: *A palace scene in which the Naga King Varuna (with his son by his side) is talking to his daughter and wife about Purnaka's proposal of marriage to Irandati. The thoughtful concern of the young prince is very realistically conveyed. The bolster behind the king provides valuable information for the study of textile design used in ancient India.*

RIGHT: *A detail of a scene set in a balcony of the Naga King Varuna's palace, with Queen Vimala talking to her daughter Irandati. They are discussing the prospect of the marriage of the princess with the brave Yaksha general Purnaka. An abashed Irandati has placed her forefinger on her chin, indicating sentiments of modesty in contemplation of her marriage.*

On the left Purnaka is depicted before
King Dhananjaya at the court of
Indraprastha. He shows the king a
beautiful jewel and lures him into the
game of dice (portrayed on the right).
This is the dramatic turning-point
when the dice has been thrown by the
king and he has lost his beloved
minister to Purnaka.

King Dhananjaya is depicted on the left, having lost his minister Vidhurapandita (painted in the middle) to Purnaka, who is seated on the right. The unhappy king is asking his wise minister whether, under the terms of the wager, the good minister could be considered the king's property and therefore would now have to be handed over to Purnaka. The honest minister replies that he has indeed become the property of Purnaka.

The wise minister Vidhurapandita, seen here holding a lotus (a symbol of his
divine nature), is delivering a discourse to the ladies of the court of Indraprastha,
before he sets forth with his new master Purnaka.

In the detail opposite several of the ladies of the court are shown. This graceful
maiden holding a flower in her hand appears mournful as the minister will soon be
taking his leave of them.

On the left Vidhurapandita teaches the sacred doctrine to the Naga King Varuna, who is depicted with a halo of five serpent hoods, symbolic of his race. Beside the Naga king are two ladies, probably his wife Vimala and daughter Irandati. Purnaka is seen behind the Bodhisattva, seated on a cushion with a check pattern.

In the upper right corner Queen Vimala is seen on a balcony with Irandati as they discuss the prospect of her marriage to Purnaka. Below the balcony a man and a woman are shown in conversation The man's features and the lotus in his hand indicate that this is the Bodhisattva Vidhurapandita. Queen Vimala, who is deeply impressed by his wisdom, listens to him.

RIGHT: *The ceiling outside the antechamber to the main shrine (for a detail of the figures in the bottom right corner see* p. 140). *Geometric patterns are a prominent feature of all the ceiling decorations in this cave.*

OPPOSITE: *Detail of the painted ceiling in the rear aisle. Despite the considerably darkened effect caused by soot deposits and shellac, the decorative painting is remarkable for its beautiful floral motifs and geese drawn in prolific variety. The geometric designs on the sides are exceptional; they are reminiscent of similar decorative patterns used in ancient Greek art. The skilful shading gives a three-dimensional effect to these patterns.*

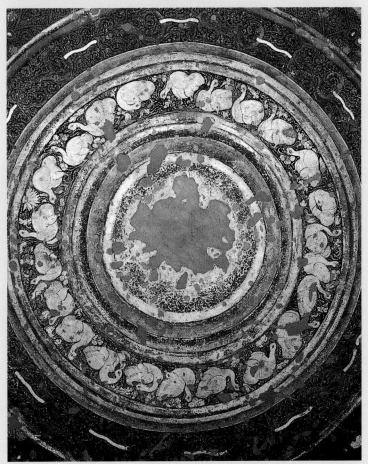

RIGHT: *Decorative design painted on the ceiling of the left-hand chapel, featuring a circular band filled with geese in various attitudes.*

BELOW: *A detail from the ceiling just outside the antechamber to the main shrine (see p. 139, above). Such flying celestial figures, with flowers and geometric designs, cover the entire expanse of the ceiling.*

A detail from the ceiling of the main shrine. A gana (cherub) floating amid clouds, brings offerings of flowers to the Buddha. There are four such ganas, one in each corner of the ceiling. The drawing of their bodies is very refined and has parallels in the plump cherubs depicted in Renaissance art in Europe.

LEFT: *An* arhat *(a highly evolved intellectual being on the True Path) seen flying through the air amid white clouds; he carries flowers and fruits, perhaps as an offering to the Buddha.*

Two details from the painted ceiling of the verandah.

ABOVE: *Two men who, from the markings on their foreheads, appear to be priests, are drinking together. Their postures are bent and ungainly, perhaps on account of their inebriated state. Both are very fastidious in their attire. Of particular interest are the matching blue and white head-dress, scarves and socks of the man on the left.*

LEFT: *A panel with beautifully painted lotuses; the brilliant blue of the lapis luzuli contrasts most effectively with the predominantly white flowers. The lotus motif is widely used in Buddhist and Hindu art. It is symbolic of purity for, though it rises from even the muddiest waters, the lotus flower always retains its own brilliant beauty.*

Cave 16

Some six hundred years after the first group of Hinayana caves were excavated, Ajanta again bursts forth into creative activity. A donation is made by Varahadeva, a minister of the Vakataka King Harisena, for the making of the grand *vihara* now known as Cave 16.

The Vakatakas were a powerful Hindu dynasty who ruled over the central Deccan in the fifth and early sixth centuries AD. They had no religious prejudices, and many beautiful Buddhist caves which represent much of the finest art of Ajanta were created during their times.

Varahadeva, who was a devout Buddhist and was also responsible for the excavation of other caves, dedicated this cave dwelling to the Buddhist Samgha in remembrance of his parents. It was to be 'adorned with windows, doors, rows of beautiful pictures, ledges, statues of celestial nymphs and the like, and supported by beautiful pillars, and with a temple of Buddha inside' (translation by Dr V. V. Mirashi). Cave 16 is ascribed to the end of the fifth century, during the rule of King Harisena, at whose court Varahadeva was a minister.

From the river the visitor climbs up steps, through a magnificent gateway flanked by large sculpted elephants (right) to reach this grand vihara. It has a large verandah, 65 ft (19.80 m) in length and 10 ft 8 in. (3.25 m) wide. The hall has twenty columns and a gallery which runs all around it. The front gallery, 74 ft (22.55 m) in length, is a little longer than the one at the rear of the hall. The shrine in the back of the cave has no antechamber and is entered directly from the gallery. For a plan of this cave see p. 236.

Although most of the paintings in this cave have been destroyed, those that remain show a very high degree of development in style and speak of a truly inspired period in the creation of the Ajanta site.

A detail from the Maha–Ummagga Jataka, *which is about the Bodhisattva who, in the form of a seven-year-old child called Mahasodha, preached the Law. Here we see variously attired persons listening with rapt attention to the discourse of the Bodhisattva.*

On the left-hand wall of the cave, a few
patches of the original paintings remain,
including the two dancing figures shown
here. The postures and gestures of the
hands as depicted appear to be very similar
to those of the performing arts still practised
in India.

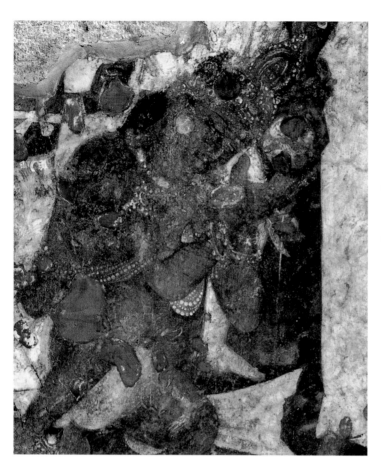

Details from the story of the 'Conversion of Nanda' by the Buddha

(see also pp. 78–81).

LEFT: *The richly bejewelled and crowned Prince Nanda receiving the Buddha, who has come before him. The reverence and gentle expression on his face is the hallmark of the compassionate art of Ajanta, which always manages to portray great depth of inner feeling.*

BELOW AND OPPOSITE: *Nanda sits on the floor in a monastery as he has his head shaved by a barber on joining the holy Order. The painted area showing the upper part of the body of the barber has flaked off, but the inclination of Nanda's head confirms the scene. A monk is also present watching the operation.*

Having had his head shaved on becoming a bhikshu, *Prince Nanda is depicted here in a disconsolate mood, suffering the pangs of separation from his beautiful wife. Other monks are also present in the pavilion.*

The forlorn Princess Janapadakalyani is pining away because her husband Nanda has left her to become an ascetic. About this scene, which is called the 'Dying Princess', Griffiths, who spent thirteen years painting reproductions of Ajanta murals, has written: 'For pathos and sentiment and the unmistakable way of telling its story this picture cannot be surpassed in the history of art.'

In the top right corner two palace maids are shown discussing the sad condition of the queen. Interestingly, one of them has woolly hair (possibly a negroid characteristic) and the other wears a scarf, the style of which suggests that she may be either Parthian or Scythian.

Cave 17

After Cave 16, this magnificent *vihara* was the next great cave to be created at Ajanta. An inscription here records the fact that it was donated by a feudatory of King Harisena and dates it to the end of the fifth century.

In this splendid cave the walls are adorned with a profusion of painted stories. The *Simhala Avadana* and the *Visvantara Jataka,* depicted in all the complexity of their numorous incidents, each stretching across about 45 ft (13.70 m) of wall space, are truly magnificent murals conceived on a vast and impressive scale.

If the paintings in Cave 1 depict the magnificence of palace scenes and courtly elegance, the stories in this *vihara* also take us deep into the realm of Nature, with its forests and animals. Among the *Jatakas* depicted here are numerous stories of earlier births of the Buddha in the form of various animals, including a monkey, a deer, a buffalo and an elephant. The all-pervading compassion of Buddhism and its respect for all animal life are constantly with us in this cave, where there is no distinction at all between men and animals.

The *vihara* is similar in plan to Cave 16, but it has an antechamber to the shrine. The front verandah measures 64 ft x 9 ft 10 in. (19.50 x 3.00 m). The main hall, which is 64 ft (19.50 cm) square, has three entrances and twenty beautifully painted pillars. The shrine measures 18 ft x 19 ft 6 in. (5.50 x 5.94 m) and is preceded by a large antechamber.

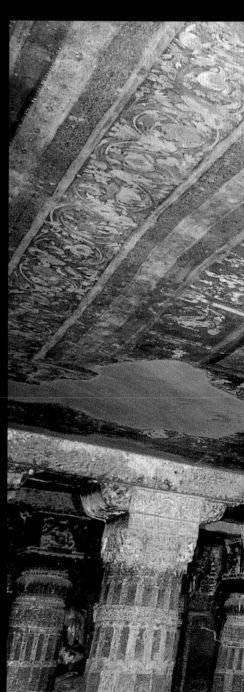

A view of the magnificently painted interior of Cave 17. Originally, almost the entire surface of the walls and ceiling was painted. The ceiling features skilfully executed undulations to suggest the cloth canopy of a shamiana (decorated tent).

Visvantara Jataka *The fruits of generosity*

This is one of the most popular *Jatakas* in Buddhist lore. At Ajanta, it has been painted in vivid and sensitive detail in two places in Cave 17: on the wall of the verandah and inside on the left wall of the cave. See pp. 159–64 and 186–91.

The Bodhisattva was born to King Sanjaya and Queen Phusati in the city of Jetuttara as Prince Visvantara. This was his last birth before he achieved Enlightenment and became the Buddha. As was predicted at the time of his birth, Prince Visvantara was very generous and distributed all that he possessed to the needy.

Once, when the neighbouring kingdom of Kalinga was in the grip of a severe drought, the benevolent Prince decided to alleviate the suffering of the people by giving away a precious and magical elephant which brought rain to his own kingdom. The citizens of Jetuttara were incensed and threatened to revolt against the king unless he banished the prince. Visvantara responded immediately and left the palace with his wife Princess Madri and their two children, Prince Jali and Princess Kanhajina. Before leaving, he called the people and distributed alms amongst them. He even gave away the horses and the chariot which he was to use to leave the kingdom.

In order to test Prince Visvantara's virtue of generosity to its very limit, the Gods presented before him a cruel Brahmin called Jujuka, who appeared as an old and feeble man and asked him for his children so that they might serve him and alleviate his suffering. Although this gesture was extremely painful to him, the benovolent Prince agreed and gave his children to the Brahmin. Jujuka beat and ill-treated the children for fourteen days until (guided by the designs of the Gods) he took them into the city of Jetuttara. There they were recognized by the king's men, who took the Brahmin and the children to King Sanjaya's court.

The king was overjoyed to see his grandchildren again and paid Jujuka the handsome ransom demanded by him for their release. The people of Jetuttara and the king felt deeply remorseful for having banished their virtuous prince. Visvantara and Madri were summoned from their hermitage deep in the forest and reunited with their children amidst great celebration.

A detail from the Visvantara Jataka *painted on the wall of the verandah, to the left of the entrance. Mendicants are gathered to receive alms. Of particular interest is the small square-shaped umbrellas held by two of them.*

OVERLEAF: *Palace scene from the* Visvantara Jataka *painted in the verandah (see also details on pp. 162–3). Part of the decorative ceiling is also shown.*

Two details from the palace pavilion scenes. Prince Visvantara has been banished from the kingdom and is seen walking out of the palace gate (left). Behind him is very fine depiction of a areca-nut tree. His wife Princess Madri follows (above). There is a fascinating depiction of two persons watching from a window. Using a most interesting device to convey the reduced light of the interior, the artist has painted these individuals in monochrome.

The Vedic deity Lord Indra descends from the clouds with celestial musicians to observe Prince Visvantara. (He is referred to very often in Buddhist legends.) On the right a female flautist in a delightful pose is seen from behind. The treatment of the ribbons in her hair provides yet another example of the rich variety of contemporary hair-styles.

Two apsaras (celestial beings) paying obeisance. One of them has placed her hand on the shoulder of the other in a refreshingly natural way. This ease and happy familiarity is also often seen in Indian sculptures contemporary with the Ajanta caves.

*One of the most refined painted figures in all of Ajanta: a flying apsara painted
on the wall of the verandah, to the right of the doorway. The artist has followed
the rules of the* Vishnudharmottara *closely, and we thus see the jewellery of her
chic turban, the strings of pearls in her necklace and her scarves moving in the wind
as she flies amidst the clouds. She appears to be the epitome of sophistication and
fashion. The narrow eyebrows appear to be outlined in much the same way as is
done today and her earrings seem to anticipate modern styles*

The Buddha and the elephant Nalagiri

The Buddha's envious cousin Devadatta conspired many times to kill the Great Being, but without success. In his third attempt, the evil Devadatta, together with King Ajatashatru of Rajagraha, planned an attack on the Buddha. They took a ferocious elephant named Nalagiri and made him drunk with liquor. The intoxicated elephant was released on the streets of Rajagraha, just when the Buddha was passing through. The elephant charged through the streets, wreaking destruction in his path. However, when he came before the Buddha, the Enlightened One gently raised his hand to halt him. Despite his maddened state, Nalagiri recognized the loving kindness emanating from the Buddha and immediately knelt down before him in obeisance.

The Buddha stroked Nalagiri's head, and the elephant was tamed forever by this display of compassionate love.

On the wall of the verandah, to the right of the beautiful apsaras, is painted the story of Nalagiri, the maddened elephant. In the first part of this narrative Devadatta is seen conspiring with King Ajatashatru of Rajagraha, depicted in the upper balcony of a palace. Below them are people in the palace who are visibly disturbed, having heard of the evil plans being hatched.

The maddened elephant Nalagiri charging through the streets of Rajagraha. People scatter and shop-keepers are seen closing their doors, while other citizens gather on their balconies in a state of fear as they watch the chaos below.

To everybody's amazement, the crazed elephant has come and knelt at the feet of the Buddha, who lovingly strokes the animal's head. Citizens on their balconies are seen folding their hands as they gaze down on this miraculous scene.

A detail from the ceiling of the
main hall, showing two buffalo.
The lines of the recumbent animal
are particularly graceful.

A wealth of animal and mythical figures is depicted on the ceiling of the cave – a virtual encyclopaedia of the creatures featured in India's religions and folklore. (Left) A pair of deer listening to the first sermon of the Buddha at Sarnath; (right) celestial figures called kinnaras, *half-human and half-bird, in flight; (below) a rare form of* kinnara, *part-horse and part-woman.*

Shaddanta Jataka *The Story of a Six-tusked Elephant*

On the banks of a lake in the Himalayas, there lived the Bodhisattva King Elephant called Shaddanta. He was a great white elephant who had six tusks which emitted rays of light of different colours. The Bodhisattva King, who led a herd of 80,000 elephants, had two wives named Mahasubhadda and Cullasubhadda.

One day, while he and his herd visited a sal grove in which the trees were in blossom, he unintentionally offended his younger Queen Cullasubhadda by shaking the bough of a Sal tree and showering its beautiful blooms upon Queen Mahasubhadda. The sense of injury felt by the younger queen was compounded when he also presented to Mahasubhadda a large lotus with seven shoots. Cullasubhadda felt a deep grudge against him and prayed that she be reborn as Queen of Benaras so that she could take her revenge against Shaddanta.

Her wish was fulfilled. One day, as the Queen of Benaras, she feigned sickness and called the king to her side. She expressed a desire to possess the six tusks of a great white elephant who lived in a distant forest in the Himalayas. A hunter named Sonuttara was chosen to track down the elephant. He was able to trap Shaddanta and shot a poisoned arrow into him, but was unable to saw off his splendid tusks. The Bodhisattva asked Sonuttara why he needed his tusks; on being told of the queen's desire, and even though he was in great pain, the Great Elephant took the saw in his own trunk and cut off his tusks.

Sonuttara the hunter returned to Benaras and presented the brilliant white tusks to the queen. On seeing them, she suddenly recalled the magnificent elephant who had been her beloved husband in her previous birth. The queen was sickened with grief for having killed the kindly Shaddanta and died.

RIGHT: *The Shaddanta Jataka is painted on the front wall of Cave 17, on the left of the entrance. Here, the Bodhisattva Shaddanta is shown with his herd of elephants in the forest.*

The hunter kneels reverentially before the kindly Bodhisattva Shaddanta, who is removing his tusks himself and handing them over.

LEFT: *A palace scene in which the hunters are shown bringing the tusks of the Bodhisattva Shaddanta which the queen had demanded. On seeing the tusks, the queen faints.*

OPPOSITE: *A gracefully painted detail from the story of the* Shaddanta Jataka, *with a hunter and a monkey sitting under a* palasa *tree. The stones on which the monkey sits are shaped in the peculiar onventional style followed in all the paintings of the Ajanta caves, where hills, rocks and stony surfaces are depicted in stylized geometric forms.*

On one branch of the palasa *tree the artist has painted a row of ants (see p. 33). This minute attention to detail reflects the interest of the painters of Ajanta in representing all the creatures of this world.*

Hamsa Jataka *An inspiring paean to the virtues of loyalty and friendship*

This is a tale about a sacred golden goose called Dhritarashtra who lived with his flock on Mount Chitrakuta.

One day, Queen Khema of Benaras dreamt that a golden goose was preaching to her. She requested the king to ask the Brahmins in their court to find this goose so that she could hear his complete sermon. The king was told about the Bodhisattva Goose and, in order to lure Dhritarashtra and his flock to Benaras, he constructed a beautiful artificial lake, covered with many-hued lotuses. A fowler was instructed to keep watch over the lake so as to catch the golden goose when he arrived with his flock.

And so it happened that Dhritarashtra alighted on the banks of the lake and was caught in a snare set by the fowler. The Bodhisattva

The flock of geese takes flight, having been warned in time by the Bodhisattva King Dhritarashtra. In the lower part of this scene the hunter bears the Bodhisattva Golden Goose and his minister Sumukha on his shoulders. A detail showing the loyal minister appears on p. 185.

Goose waited patiently till the flock had eaten their fill, then uttered a cry of warning to them. All the geese flew away except for his minister Sumukha. The Bodhisattva entreated Sumukha to make good his escape, but he refused. When the fowler witnessed this unusual sight, he took both geese to the royal court.

The king was deeply impressed when he heard the story of the loyalty of the two geese, and both of them were received at court with great honours. Then, as the Queen had dreamt, the Bodhisattva Goose preached the Law of Dharma to the royal couple.

The court of King Samyama and Queen Khema in Benaras. The hunter who has brought the Bodhisattva Golden Goose and his minister Sumukha tells the king about the rare display of courage and loyalty on the part of Sumukha, who had allowed himself to be caught, refusing to leave the side of his leader.

OPPOSITE: *The minister Sumukha.*

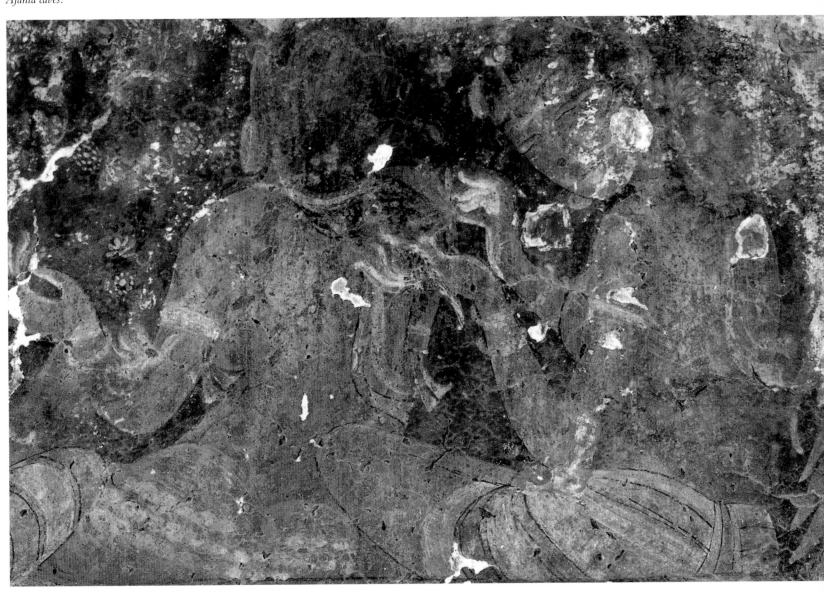

A detail from the story showing Princess Madri as she and her husband give alms to the people.

The glance of compassion. In this scene — truly one of the great masterpieces of the art of Ajanta — two men look compassionately towards the prince and princess as they depart from the city, having been banished, giving away all that they possess.

OPPOSITE: *The evil Brahmin Jujuka who took away the children of Visvantara and Madri and demanded a large ransom for their return.*

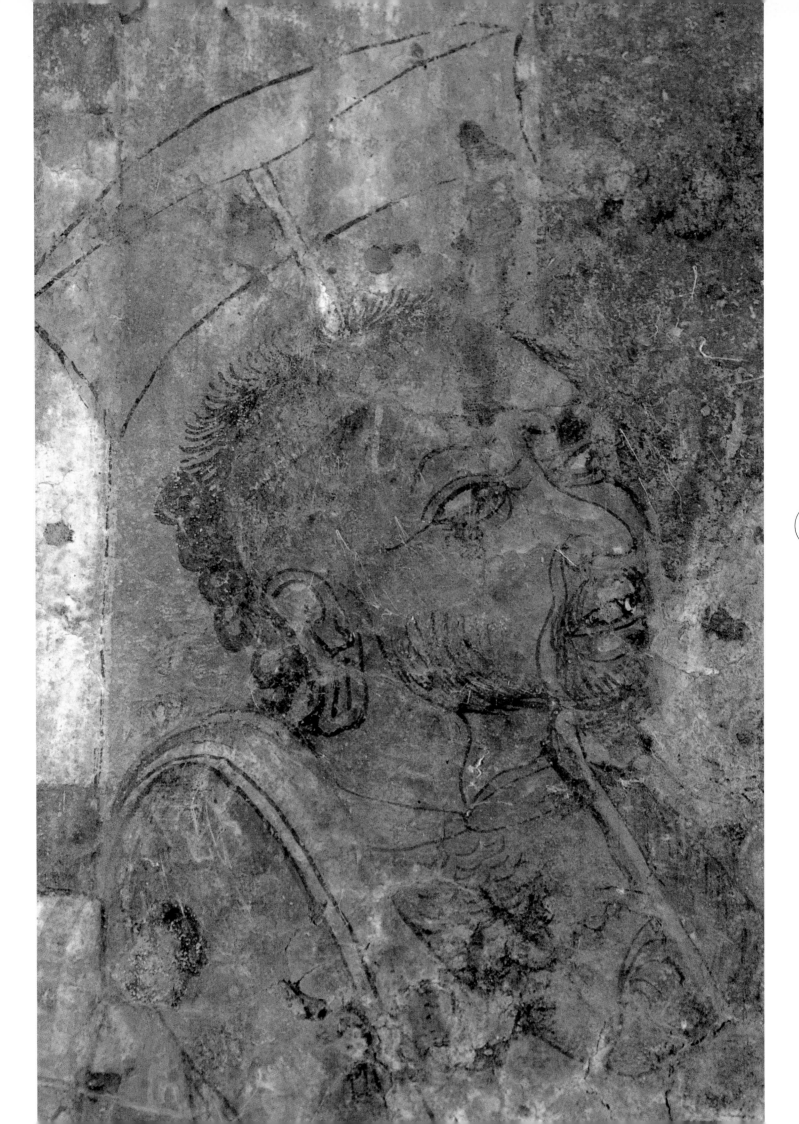

The story ends happily with the abhishek *(ritual bath) of Prince Visvantara, after the prince and princess have been accepted back into the palace.*

A detail from the previous scene shows Princess Madri looking on from a small palace pavilion. The awkwardness in the lines of the face, the necklace and the limbs is evidence of later repainting. Close study of the murals of Cave 17 may yield further valuable information about the historic development of the site.

A beautiful painting of a yaksha (celestial being) bearing an offering of fruits, on a pilaster on the left wall of the cave.

Kapi Jataka *A tale of ingratitude and its consequences*

King Brahmadutta, who ruled over Benaras, was once on the road to a pleasant park called Migacira. On his way he came upon a Brahmin afflicted with leprosy, who was lying on the ground in agony. The king stopped and asked him the reason for his woeful state. The Brahmin then told him the story of the misdeeds which had brought him to this pitiable end.

One day, when he was collecting some delicious fruits in the forest, he fell into a pit which was too deep for him to climb out of. As he lay at the bottom, he was spotted by a monkey who was in fact the Great Being in one of his previous births.

Recognizing the man's plight, the kindly Bodhisattva climbed down and brought the man out of the pit, carrying him on his back Exhausted by his efforts, the monkey decided to rest Meanwhile, the man felt hungry and decided to kill the monkey and eat him. He picked up a rock and threw it at the monkey's head. Injured and bleeding, after being so rudely awakened, the monkey admonished the man for his ingratitude.

The kindly Bodhisattva then showed the man the way out of the forest. On their way they came across a lake, where he washed his bleeding wound. The man was thirsty and drank some water from the lake. As he drank the water, pustules broke out on his body, for 'According to his deeds each man doth fare'. And so he suffered from leprosy and was shunned by all the people in the town where he lived.

The Bodhisattva Monkey finds a man who has fallen into a pit and is trapped.

While the exhausted monkey is asleep, the man throws a rock at his head in order to kill him, for he is hungry. The injured Bodhisattva Monkey, seen on the left, below, is shown admonishing the man for being so ungrateful.

Sutasoma Jataka *A story of cannibal habits*

In one of his previous births, the Buddha lived as Sutasoma, a son of the King of Indraprastha. He studied at the famous centre of learning, Takasila, and in time ascended the throne of Indraprastha. Among his fellow students was Prince Saudasa, who later became King of Benaras.

In his previous birth Saudasa had been a *yaksha* and was unable to give up his desire to eat human flesh. As king, he began to feed his cannibal appetite by having his own subjects murdered. Eventually the citizens drove Saudasa out of Benaras with the help of the army.

The cannibal Saudasa then lived in the forest and preyed upon travellers. One day, when Sutasoma had gone into the forest to bathe in a lotus pool, Saudasa attacked him and took him prisoner. Sutasoma requested the cannibal to free him for just one day so that he may hear 'the four holy verses' from a sage, after which he would return.

When Sutasoma kept his promise and came back the next day, Saudasa was greatly impressed by the Bodhisattva's truthfulness and courage. The Enlightened One then preached the Law of Dharma to Saudasa, who gave up cannibalism and took to a gentle way of life.

(In the mural of Cave 17, a different reason for the cannibal tendencies of Prince Saudasa is depicted. Here, his father – the King of Benaras – is seen taking a nap in the forest. While he sleeps, a lioness who is deeply attracted to him comes and licks his feet. According to the story as delineated here, in this manner the lioness becomes pregnant with his child who is later born as Saudasa. Saudasa leads a normal life until one day he unknowingly gets a taste of human flesh. Thereafter the lioness's blood in him takes over and he develops a cannibal appetite.)

The Sutasoma Jataka *is painted on the rear wall of the cave to the left of the* *antechamber and continues beyond the corner onto the left wall. Here, the lioness* *is shown at the royal court, telling the king that she is carrying his child.*

196

On the death of his father, Prince Saudasa succeeds him as King of Benaras. In this scene his abhishek (ritual bath) on ascending the throne is depicted.

The palace kitchen. One day the cook makes the mistake of serving human flesh to the king, without realizing what a profound effect it would have upon him.

The king happily eats his meal of human flesh.

ABOVE: *In the thick of the battle scene when the army rises in revolt against the king: cavalry and foot-soldiers in the confusion of war.*

LEFT: *A detail of the battle scene: King Saudasa. A fine painting with excellent depiction of the king's horse and the movement of its forelegs*

The Buddha has come before his wife Yashodhara and their son Rahula. Yashodhara has tutored the child to ask Him for his rightful inheritance, being born the son of a prince, but the Buddha says he has only his begging bowl to offer.

Owing to his spiritual importance, the Buddha is depicted here as a much larger figure, towering over Yashodhara and Rahula, who are also shown in detail (right). Despite considerable damage to the paintings, the masterly depiction of the emotions of the mother and child are still vividly seen.

Rahula, who looks up adoringly at his father, presents a very human and realistic portrait. Yashodhara has bedecked herself profusely with jewellery to induce her husband to stay with her. This attempt to entice him is enhanced by the stray curl of hair falling on her right shoulder. The highlights on Yashodhara's figure, particularly along the entire right side, have been used in much the same way as side-lighting is used in photography today to enhance the rounded form of the human body.

Scenes painted on the left wall of the antechamber of the shrine. It is believed that the Buddha miraculously ascended to heaven to preach to his mother Mahamaya, who had passed away seven days after his birth.

BELOW: *A group of women are shown listening to the Buddha's discourse in the Tushita Heaven.*

RIGHT: *A detail from the scene representing the descent of the Buddha from heaven, which is painted in the middle of the mural: crowned and beautifully attired* Devas *(gods and celestial beings) have come before him in attitudes of devotion.*

In the lower section of the mural, the Buddha is shown after returning to earth. Many rajas, ranis and chiefs, riding on richly caparisoned elephants and horses, have come to pay their respects to the Master and to learn the Doctrine from him. See line drawing on p. ooo

LEFT: *A detail of the assembly gathered around the Buddha. The king in the centre is likely to be Bimbisara of Rajagraha, who was the first royal patron of the Enlightened One. On the left are two figures on horseback who appear to be foreigners, perhaps from countries to the north-west of India. One of them is bearded whilst the other has a twisted moustache. In front of them are two more foreigners wearing round fur-brimmed caps. It may be remembered that before the period when these paintings were executed Gandhara and other provinces to the north-west of India had come under the influence of Buddhism.*

RIGHT: *On the right-hand wall of the antechamber of the shrine are portrayed some of the sceptics before whom the Buddha performed the miracle of Shravasti. Here we see a guru (spiritual teacher) supported by his followers. In a satirical moment, the artist ridicules the hypocrisy of such obese 'ascetics' and their teacher who is barely able to support his own weight.*

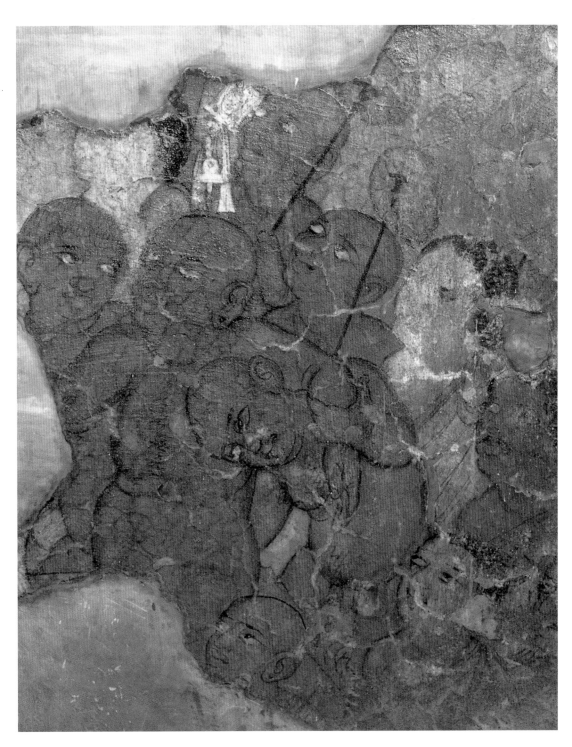

Matriposhaka Jataka
The loyalty of a son towards his blind mother

Once during the reign of King Brahmadutta of Benaras, the Bodhisattva was born as a white elephant who lived in the Himalayas. He had a blind mother whom he looked after with loving care.

One day he found a forester who had lost his way and the kindly Bodhisattva, having gently placed him on his back, took him out of the forest. The forester was deeply impressed by the beauty of this white elephant, who he thought would greatly please the King of Benaras. With this wicked purpose in mind, he marked the trees along the path that they took out of the forest. On reaching Benaras, he heard that the royal elephant had died. Sensing a fortunate opportunity to please the king, the forester led his men to Mount Chadorana, where the Bodhisattva lived. The Great Being allowed himself to be captured, as he did not wish to fight and hurt the men.

On seeing the beautiful elephant, the king was overjoyed. A special stable was prepared for him and the choicest food was placed before him. To the amazement of all, the Bodhisattva refused to eat. The king entreated him, saying:

'Come, take a morsel, Elephant and never pine away:

There's many a thing to serve your King that you shall do one day.'

(translated by R.A. Neil, edited by E.B. Cowell).

But the Elephant replied, 'Without my mother, I will eat nothing'… and he told the king about his blind mother who would be helpless without him.

The king was deeply impressed by the Bodhisattva Elephant's loyalty to his blind mother and therefore granted him his freedom. The happy Elephant then returned to his mother, who blessed the king for having given her son back to her.

The Matriposhaka Jataka *is painted on the rear wall of the cave, to the right of the antechamber. (The artist has taken the liberty of painting two blind parents instead of the blind mother of the Bodhisattva Elephant.)*

LEFT: *The Bodhisattva White Elephant is led by the hunter to the palace of the King of Benaras.*

BELOW: *The reunion of the Bodhisattva Elephant with his parents. He pours water on his mother's head and trumpets joyfully. Great feeling is displayed in the painting, in which the blind parents are shown fondly caressing their son with their trunks.*

Mahisha Jataka *The fate of a mischievous monkey*

A detail of the Mahisha Jataka, painted on the right-hand wall of the cave. Although the monkey is troubling the Bodhisattva Buffalo, he takes it in a kindly spirit.

In one of his previous births, the Buddha was born as a Bodhisattva Buffalo who lived in the Himalayas.

An impertinent monkey used to trouble and tease the buffalo often. The kindly Bodhisattva, however, tolerated the monkey's bad behaviour patiently and did not respond angrily.

As it came to pass, a savage buffalo was standing one day under the same tree where the Bodhisattva used to be. Mistaking him for the kindly buffalo, the mischievous monkey played his usual pranks on him. This buffalo, however, immediately threw the monkey on the ground and, despite the monkey's pleading and entreaties, trampled upon him and killed him.

OPPOSITE: *The monkey is in trouble. Unwittingly, he has teased another buffalo, who has reacted as one would expect; this buffalo has thrown down the impertinent monkey, who is seen pleading that he should not be trampled upon.*

Simhala Avadana

In the kingdom of Simhakalpa ruled by King Simhakesri, there lived a rich merchant called Simhaka. He had a courageous son called Simhala. One day, Simhala requested that his father allow him to go on a sea voyage with other merchants. His father tried to dissuade him, saying that the journey was treacherous and that he would have to undergo many hardships and dangers on the way. However, seeing that Simhala had set his heart on the voyage, he reluctantly allowed him to leave.

Unfortunately, Simhaka's fears were realized. Simhala and his fellow merchants were shipwrecked and cast upon the shores of the island of Tamradvipa. The island was inhabited by cannibalistic ogresses, who came to the merchants disguised as beautiful women. At first they lured the merchants with their charms, but at night turned into ogresses to devour them.

As it transpired, the Bodhisattva, who was born as a magical white horse named Bahala, was flying over the island. Seeing the sad predicament of the merchants, he was filled with compassion and offered to take them to the safety of their kingdom in Jambudvipa (as India was then known). Simhala and 250 merchants clung to the magical horse, which bore them away to safety. The others were devoured by the ogresses.

In the meantime, one ogress came to the palace of King Simhakesri, bringing a child with her. She claimed that the child was Simhala's and that he had abandoned her. When the king questioned Simhala, he denied the story and warned his father that the woman was actually an ogress in disguise. The king, however, was enchanted by her beauty and took her into his harem.

Having tricked her way into the royal palace, the ogress now summoned her friends from Tamradvipa. Together, they killed the king and all the inhabitants of the palace.

Amid great sadness and fear, the people called upon the brave Simhala to take the throne. He then led a large army into Tamradvipa and defeated the ogresses in a great battle. The island was then colonized by him and was renamed Simhaladvipa.

The Simhala Avadana *is depicted on a grand scale and covers almost all of the right-hand wall of the cave. Because this mural is better preserved than many others, it is possible to present the* Avadana *with many interesting details of the narrative.*

In the lower portion of the panel is a shipwreck scene (left). Five hundred merchants led by Simhala are cast ashore on an island. The ogresses who inhabit it come forward in the guise of beautiful women to charm the merchants (below).

A large section of the Simhala
Avadana (above) reveals the narrative
structure on the wall. In the mid-
section we see many of the merchants
who have been beguiled by ogresses in
the form of attractive women. The
artist has depicted these scenes with
great zest, showing couples indulging
in revelry and sensual pleasures.

Inside a decorated pavilion (see detail,
opposite), is a merchant who has been
seduced by an ogress in the form of a
lovely woman. This delightful painting
shows what appears to be a tender and
loving moment.

Having seduced the merchants and put
them completely at ease, the ogresses
come into their true form. They attack
the men viciously with their curved
daggers and dreadful fangs.

One of the merchants, screaming in
agony, is flung over backwards. The
curve and movement of his body is
very dynamically depicted

In the meantime, the Bodhisattva Horse has arrived on the scene. The merchants fall on their knees, begging him to save them.

The Bodhisattva Horse flies off, carrying Simhala on his back. Other merchants, clinging to different parts of the horse, are also taken to safety.

The Bodhisattva Horse is greeted with reverence as he lands at Simhakalpa, bringing Simhala and the other merchants.

The court of King Simhakesri. In the bottom right corner is an ogress who has come in the guise of an attractive woman accompanied by a child.

The disguised ogress tells the king that she is the daughter of the king of the island of Tamradvipa, and that Simhala is the father of the child she has brought with her. Simhala who is depicted next to her warns the king that she is actually an ogress, but the king is so taken with her charms that he does not believe his son. Since Simhala has rejected her, the king decides to take her into his own harem.

ABOVE: *The ploy of the disguised ogress to gain entry to the king's harem having succeeded, many ogresses now come to attack the palace. Vultures follow in their wake.*

RIGHT: *The chambers of the king's harem present a gruesome sight as the ogresses attack the women and drink their blood.*

    In the middle chamber, a red ogress has caught the knot of a woman's hair and is about to cut it off with a dagger. Another ogress of pale complexion has thrown down a woman and has placed her foot upon her to hold her down. To the right, another pale ogress has plunged a dagger into the abdomen of a woman· and, having filled her cup with blood, drinks it. Two other women are seized with terror, one covering her eyes and the other holding her hands to her breast. The women in the chamber on the left are shown in a detail overleaf.

LEFT: *In the chamber on the left are three women. One has fainted at the sight of the ogresses and is being supported by her companion. The third, struck with horror, is depicted with her hand on her chin.*

BELOW: *Two ogresses in flight. The one in front holds a cup filled with human flesh and the other carries a striped cup full of blood. A crow swoops down to drink the blood from her cup.*

OPPOSITE: *Vultures, some of them shown in the act of eating bits of human flesh, are everywhere in this gruesome scene.*

OPPOSITE: *In the forecourt of the palace, guards armed with shields and naked swords are powerless to help in this dire situation.*

BELOW: *A great and powerful army assembled under Simhala's command heads towards the island of the ogresses. The crowned Simhala, who is now King of Simhakalpa, is seated* *on a white elephant. The animals have been portrayed with realistic detail, and two of the elephants are shown with their trunks intertwined as they advance.*

Sibi Jataka
Great generosity reaps its reward

In one of his previous births the Bodhisattva was King Sibi, who ruled righteously, observing the Ten Royal Virtues, in the city of Aritthapura (see also pp. 72–5).

The king was very benevolent and distributed alms generously. His munificence was such that he built six halls, one at each of the city's gates and one at his own palace, from where alms were distributed every day. The king was not content, however, for he wished to give away something that was more meaningful than just material possessions. He therefore made a vow that

'If there be any human gift that
I have never made,
Be it my eyes, I'll give it now, all
firm and unafraid.'

Sakka (the name given to Lord Indra in Buddhist lore) decided to test the king's brave resolve to make this invaluable gift to anyone who might ask for it, so he appeared before the king as a blind Brahmin and begged him to give one of his eyes:

'To ask an eye the old man comes from far,
for I have none:
O! Give me one of yours, I pray, then we
shall each have one.'

The king was overjoyed that his wish could now be fulfilled and gladly replied:

'One eye thou didst request of me, behold, I give thee two!'

(translated by R.A. Neil, edited by E.B. Cowell)

He sent for the royal servant Sivaka, who was ordered to remove his eyes and give them to the blind Brahmin. The news of the king's decision spread throughout the city and soon all his courtiers and the people gathered in the palace, pleading with him not to make this sacrifice, but to no avail. Sivaka reluctantly carried out the king's orders and removed his eyes. King Sibi, thinking that a blind king was of no use to his people, left the palace to become an ascetic.

Lord Sakka was immensely pleased with the king's charitable act. He appeared before Sibi and granted him a pair of divine eyes with which he could see 'through rock and wall, over hill and dale … a hundred leagues on every side.' King Sibi returned to his palace to rule again, and preached the Law of self-sacrifice to his people.

The Sibi Jataka is painted on the right-hand wall of Cave 17. Though it is very damaged and not much of the story is visible, the main incidents are still identifiable: they demonstrate the immense feeling with which the artist has portrayed the story.

ABOVE: *Behind the Bodhisattva, who is in great pain, a sorrowful palace maid is shown holding her head in her hands.*

RIGHT: *One of the six halls from which alms were distributed continually to all who came. The depiction of contemporary wooden architecture is a very interesting feature of this mural.*

BELOW: *Another despairing woman beats her chest and pulls her hair.*

Mriga Jataka *The tale of the golden deer*

In one of his previous births the Buddha was a deer, golden in colour and with a very sweet voice. One day, he heard a man in a river crying out for help and swam across to save him. He then set him on the path to the city of Benaras. Before they parted, the deer requested the man to keep his existence a secret and not to guide anyone to his part of the forest.

On reaching Benaras, the man heard that the king had offered a reward to anyone who could tell him about a golden deer, as his Queen Khema had dreamt of such a deer and desired that it be brought to her.

Overcome with greed, the man guided the king to the forest where the golden deer lived. The king's huntsmen caught the deer. (In the mural at Ajanta the artist has introduced a miraculous element: as a hunter tries to catch the deer, his hands fall off and are seen lying on the ground.) Just as the king was about to shoot an arrow at the golden deer, it spoke out to him. The king was enchanted by the deer's sweet voice. On hearing that the deer had been treacherously betrayed by the man whose life it had saved, the king declared that he would kill him. The kindly Bodhisattva, however, intervened and requested the king to spare the man's life.

The king then took the golden deer to the city of Benaras with great honour and requested it to give a discourse to the queen. The Bodhisattva preached the Law of Dharma to Queen Khema and to the court of Benaras.

OPPOSITE: *The King of Benaras rides into the forest to hunt for the golden deer.*

Much to everyone's amazement, the huntsman's hands fall off just as he touches the deer's antlers. The hands are seen lying on the ground in front of the Bodhisattva Deer (right).

The Bodhisattva is transported with great honour to the royal court, where he will preach the Law of Dharma to the queen.

231

OVERLEAF: *The King of Benaras rides respectfully behind the golden deer. A very interesting detail seen in this painting is the hunting dog on a leash in the foreground.*

THE PRINCIPAL PAINTED CAVES
DESCRIPTIONS AND PLANS

The four caves illustrated in the main group of colour plates (pp. 65–232) are *viharas*, or monasteries, with individual cells placed around two or three sides of a central hall which has a shrine at the rear. Walls and ceilings alike were originally covered with paintings, large areas of which have been lost or damaged. In the brief descriptions that follow, the sequence of the surviving murals follows a clockwise direction. Where paintings still exist in the verandah and main entrance, they are listed before those in the interior of the cave. The stories illustrated in the colour plates and line drawings are marked with an asterisk.

Cave 1

One of the most important rock-cut caves in India, this *vihara* dates from the late fifth century and has some of the most beautiful mural paintings and sculpture. Its plan is typical, with a porch (destroyed) giving access to a

verandah preceding the main hall; at the rear are a centrally placed antechamber and the shrine beyond. The hall has twenty finely carved and painted pillars, with an outer aisle on all four sides. Along the left and right sides and to the left and right of the antechamber at the rear of the main hall are doorways providing access to fourteen small cells. The entrances to two further chambers are at either end of the verandah, which is 64 ft (19.50 m) long, 9 ft 3 in (2.82 m) wide and 13 ft 6 in. (4.10 m) from floor to ceiling.

The main hall is square in plan, the length of each side being the same as that of the verandah. The shrine chamber at the rear of the cave measures 19 ft 6 in. (6.00 m) square.

Within Cave 1 the principal surviving narrative murals are:
* *Sibi Jataka* (on the front wall, close up to the left of the main entrance);
* the story of the conversion of King Nanda (on the front wall, beyond the *Sibi Jataka*);
  unidentified: a palace scene (in the front aisle, on the left wall);
* *Sankhapala Jataka* (on the left-hand wall, after the palace scene);
* *Mahajanaka Jataka* (on the left-hand wall, extending on to the back wall);
* unidentified, perhaps from the *Maha-Ummagga Jataka*: the presentation of four severed human heads on a salver (on the back wall, below part of the *Mahajanaka Jataka*);
* the Bodhisattva Padmapani (on the back wall, to the left of the antechamber);
* the temptation of the Buddha by Mara (in the antechamber, on the left-hand wall);
* the Bodhisattva Avalokitesvara (in the antechamber, on the back wall to the right of the entrance to the shrine);

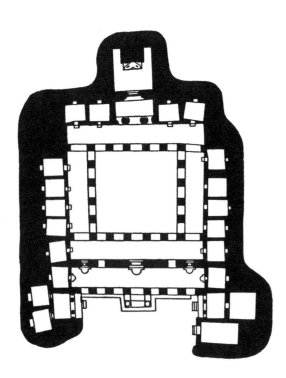

Plan of Cave 1.

the miracle of Shravasti (in the antechamber, on the right-hand wall);

the offering of lotus flowers to the Bodhisattva Vajrapani (on the back wall, to the right of the antechamber);

* *Campeya Jataka* (on the back wall, to the right of the Bodhisattva Vajrapani);

unidentified: a court scene (in the front aisle, to the right of the main entrance).

The entire ceiling of the main hall is painted with animals, birds, flowers and fruit, as well as mythological creatures and geometric designs (similar to those used in ancient Greek art).

Cave 2

This *vihara* dating from the early sixth century has a layout smilar to that of Cave 1, but its proportions are smaller. The length of the verandah is 46 ft 3 in. (14.10 m) and the sides of the roughly square main hall measure 48 ft 4 in. x 47 ft 7 in. (14.73 x 14.50 m). In the hall there are twelve massive pillars that are elaborately carved. The shrine at the rear of the cave (again preceded by an antechamber) has an imposing statue of the Buddha in the teaching posture (*dharmachakra*). There is a subsidiary chapel situated on each side of the antechamber, and there are ten cells symmetrically disposed along the left- and right-hand walls of the hall.

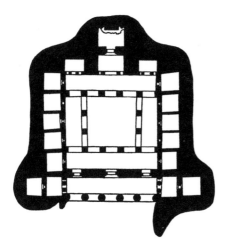

Plan of Cave 2.

The principal extant paintings are:

celestial beings (*arhats* and *kinnaras*) descending to worship a Bodhisattva (in the verandah on the back wall, to the left of the entrance);

heavenly and human worshippers bringing offerings to the Buddha (in the verandah, on the back wall, to the right of the entrance);

the god Indra and four *yakshas* (in the verandah, on the back wall, further to the right of the entrance);

Hamsa Jataka (on the front wall, on the left);

* the birth of the Buddha (on the left wall);

devotees bringing offerings (on the left- and right-hand walls of the chapel on the left);

* the Buddha depicted in numerous different attitudes (on the rear wall, between the chapel on the left and the antechamber);

* the Bodhisattva Maitreya and the Buddha in various attitudes (in the shrine chamber, to the left of the entrance);

a Bodhisattva (on the rear wall, between the antechamber and the chapel on the right);

devotees bringing offerings (on the left- and right-hand walls of the chapel on the right);

Vidhurapandita Jataka (on the right-hand wall);

Purna Avadana (on the right-hand wall);

unidentified palace scenes (on the right-hand wall in the front aisle);

various mythical beings depicted on the pedestals of the pillars enclosing the hall.

The painted decorations on the ceilings of the hall and the verandah include lotuses, geese, graceful flying celestial beings, fierce mythical creatures and floral and geometric designs.

Cave 16

This *vihara* of the fifth century is the largest of the four featured here. Its verandah is a little wider than that of Cave 1 (10 ft 8 in.; 3.25 m) but is similar in length (65 ft; 19.50 m). The main hall is, however, significantly larger, measuring 74 ft (22.25 m) at its widest end, with a ceiling height of 15 ft (4.60 m). The principal difference in plan is the absence of an antechamber to the shrine, which consists of a central chamber containing a massive figure of the Buddha, flanked by side chambers. The hall has a central main entrance and two subsidiary doorways; the internal arrangement includes twenty columns with aisles along all four sides providing access to a total of fourteen cells. Two additional chambers are situated at either end of the verandah.

This cave is notable as the only one which retains the original steps leading up to its entrance from river level.

The principal painted scenes are:
episodes from the life of the Buddha (in the verandah, on the back wall to the left of the entrance);
Sutasoma Jataka (in the verandah, above the pillars at the front);
demons in front of a monastery (on the front wall, above the left-hand door);
Hasti Jataka (on the front wall, further to the left);
* *Maha-Ummagga Jataka* (in the front aisle on the left-hand wall and a pilaster);
* the dying princess (on the left-hand wall);
* the conversion of Nanda (on the left-hand wall, further to the right);

figures of Manushi Buddhas (on the left wall, further to the right);
apsarasas and the Buddha in the teaching posture (on the left wall);
the Buddha in the teaching posture (on the back wall, to the left of the shrine);
procession of elephants (on the back wall, to the left of the entrance to the shrine);
the Buddha preaching (on the back wall, to the right of the entrance to the shrine);
scenes from the life of the Buddha (on the right-hand wall);
scenes from the early life of the future Buddha (on the right-hand wall, near the front of the cave);
a palace scene: the birth of the Buddha(?) (on the right-hand wall, near the front of the cave).

Regrettably, the state of preservation of most of the paintings in this cave is poor, making it difficult to illustrate many of the stories depicted because of the extent of the damaged areas.

Cave 17

Slightly later in date than Cave 16, this *vihara* still has many murals that have survived in a fair state of preservation. The plan is similar, with a square hall containing twenty columns, preceded by a verandah, which is 64 ft (19.50 m) long. This cave has a large antechamber measuring 18 ft 4 in. (5.60 m) across leading to the shrine, which is squarish but slightly irregular in plan (18 ft 4 in. x 19 ft 8 in.; 5.60 x 6.00 m). It contains a colossal Buddha figure in the teaching posture. There are a total of seventeen cells distributed around three sides of the hall, and a cell at each end of the verandah.

The principal narrative murals and other decorative paintings in this cave are:
* *Visvantara Jataka* (in the verandah, on the back wall towards the left) – see also pp. 176–81;
* the god Indra and *apsarasas* (in the verandah, on the back wall, to the left of the doorway);

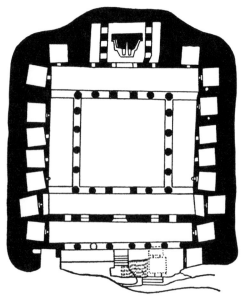

Plan of Cave 16.

* rows of Manushi Buddha figures and pairs of lovers (in the verandah, above the doorway);
* *apsarasas* and *gandharas* (in the verandah, to the right of the doorway);
* the calming of the maddened elephant Nalagiri by the Buddha (in the verandah, further to the right);

  the Bodhisattva Avalokitesvara (in the verandah, on the front wall);

  a *yaksha* with attendant (at the left end of the verandah);

  a hunt scene (at the left end of the verandah, to the left of the cell door);

  the wheel of *Samsara* (on the left wall of the verandah, above the door to the cell);

  a mother and child appearing before the Buddha (in the verandah, on either side of the second window to the right of the main entrance);

  the Buddha preaching (on the right-hand wall of the verandah, above the door to the cell);

  ceiling decorations in the verandah, featuring floral and other motifs.

The ceiling of the main hall is exquisitely painted to resemble a *shamiana* (see pp. 156–7). The principal wall paintings in the main hall and the antechamber to the shrine are:
* *Shaddanta Jataka* (on the front wall, to the left of the main entrance);
* *Mahakapi Jataka* (on the front wall, to the left of the entrance);

  Hasti Jataka (on the front wall, to the left of the entrance);

  a court scene (in the front aisle, above the cell door on the left);
* *Hamsa Jataka* (in the front aisle, on the left wall and extending on to the pilaster adjacent to it);
* *Visvantara Jataka* (on the left wall);
* *Kapi Jataka* (on the rear wall, on the left);
* *Sutasoma Jataka* (on the rear wall, to the left of the entrance to the antechamber);
* the Buddha preaching in the Tushita Heaven and after

descending to earth (in the antechamber, on the left wall);
* the Buddha and his wife and son (in the antechamber, to the left of the entrance to the shrine);

  the miracle of Shravasti (in the antechamber, on the right-hand wall);

  Sarabha Jataka (on the rear wall, to the right of the antechamber);
* *Matriposhaka Jataka* (on the rear wall, to the right);

  Matsya Jataka (on the rear wall, to the right);

  Mahisha Jataka (on the rear wall, to the right);

  Syama Jataka (in the rear aisle);
* *Simhala Avadana* (extending along the right-hand wall);
* a lady holding a mirror (on the pilaster between the right front aisles) – see p. 48;
* *Sibi Jataka* (on the pilaster at the junction of the right-hand and front aisles, continuing on the wall of the front aisle);
* *Mriga Jataka* (on the front wall, to the right of the entrance);

  Nigrodhamiga Jataka (on the front wall, to the right).

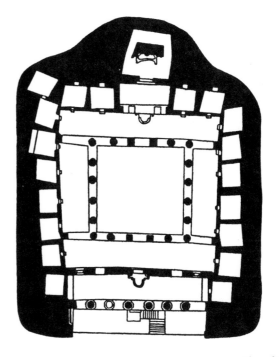

Plan of Cave 17.

APPENDIX
EARLY DESCRIPTIONS OF THE AJANTA CAVES AND THEIR DISCOVERY

AUTHOR'S NOTE

The following accounts are the most lively and interesting of those written by early visitors to the caves. However, due to the writers' lack of complete familiarity with Buddhist history and religious practices, some of their observations are not accurate.

Extracts from *TRANSACTIONS OF THE ROYAL ASIATIC SOCIETY OF GREAT BRITAIN AND IRELAND*, Vol. II (1830),

pp. 362–70:

Notice of a Visit to the Cavern Temples of Adjunta in the East-Indies.—Communicated by Lieutenant JAMES EDW. ALEXANDER, 16th Lancers, of the order of the Lion and Sun, M.R.A.S., Cor. Mem. S.A.E., &c.

Read February 7, 1829.

It was in the month of February 1824 that, while on leave from my regiment, and travelling about the province of Berar, I visited the extraordinary excavations of Adjunta, situated in lat. 20° 25' N. and lon. 76° 12' E. These, though I believe hitherto undescribed, are as much deserving of a separate publication as the far-famed temples of Ellora [situated some 70 miles to the south-west]; and though I spent only a few hours in their gloomy recesses, yet I saw enough to convince me that they are well worthy of a more minute investigation, and a lengthened sojourn amongst them.

After passing the night in a well built caravanserai in the town of Adjunta★ [original footnote: ★ From the Sanscrit word *Ajayanti*, meaning the difficult or impregnable pass.] situated at the head of the pass of the same name through one of the Berar ranges of mountains, I mounted early in the morning, arrayed in my Muselmani costume, and accompanied by a couple of servants and a guide, all of us well armed with sabres, pistols, and hunting spears. We rode through a crowd of camels with their tinkling bells, and Bunjari bullocks, reposing beside their loads of grain and salt. In passing a small party of the Nizam's horse, the Duffadar (an inferior officer) saluted us with the customary compliment of "*Salam alicum*" (Peace be with you); and enquired where we were going. I told him we proposed visiting the caves: to which he replied, "*La illah illilah!* (There is but one God) you will never return: for if you escape the tigers, these stony-hearted robbers, the Bheels, will destroy you." To this I answered, "*Inshallah* (please God) we'll have the pleasure of smoking a pipe with you in the evening." He replied, "*Khoda hafiz*" (may the Lord preserve you): and taking leave of him, we rode out of the gate which led to the head of the pass, down which our road lay.

After travelling some distance along a stony road, and passing several cairns, near which were many bushes covered with rags, pointing out the spot where unfortunate travellers had been destroyed by tigers, we suddenly found ourselves at the top of the precipitous *ghat* or pass. . . . We now dismounted, and leading our horses down a precipitous pathway to the left of the pass, found ourselves at the bottom among sweet-smelling kuskus grass. Directing our steps towards an opening between the deeply serrated hills, we arrived at the *débouche* of the glen, and fell in with a mountain stream, along whose banks lay the pathway to the caves, leading through low underwood interspersed with trees and water-grass fifteen feet in height; amongst which, not long before, three tigers had been killed.

We had not advanced far up the glen, when a low whistling was heard above us to the left, and was quickly repeated from the opposite cliffs. This proved to be Bheels intimating to one another that strangers were approaching. The guide evinced strong symptoms of fear; but on being remonstrated with, and encouraged with the hope of a handsome present, he proceeded onwards.

Some of the Bheels shewed themselves, peeping out from behind the rocks. They were a most savage looking race, perfectly black, low in stature, and nearly naked. They seemed to be armed with bows and arrows. The principal haunts of these Bheels are in the Northern Deccan, along the course of the Nerbuddah. They live entirely in the jungles, are in a state of great barbarism, and subsist by hunting, rapine, and plunder. They sometimes approach the towns and villages in the neighbourhood of their haunts, and lurk about the outskirts to attack individuals. . . . Our fire-arms prevented their attacking us; and we were allowed to proceed unmolested.

The glen, up which our road lay, almost to its termination, where the caves are situated, was remarkable for its picturesque beauty. It continued winding amongst the hills, which rose from the banks of the stream with a considerable acclivity, and having their sides clothed with scattered jungle. Amongst the trees I observed the *melia azadirachta* (neem), the *robinia mitis, mimosa Arabica* (babool), *bassia latifolia* (mowah), from which a spirit is distilled, *ficus religiosa* (peepul), &c. The hills, whose height was from four to five hundred feet, now began to close their wild and romantic features upon us; . . . it was with no common interest, and with my expectation intensely excited, that I viewed the "low browed" entrance to the first cave, which is not attained till a mile of the glen has been traversed. . . .

The first cave is about forty or fifty feet above the stream, and faces the south. The whole series of caves has the same aspect, but gradually ascends higher up the ridge; the central ones being about a hundred and fifty feet from the stream. The most remote one is near a bluff rock of two hundred feet of elevation, over whose brow a cascade dashes during the rains, though in the dry season the face of the cliff glistens with only a scanty rill.

The first circumstance that strikes an attentive observer of these magnificent remains of antiquity and wonders of art, who has previously visited the mythological or pantheistical excavations of Ellora, is the great want of ornamental and minute sculpture in the former, compared with the exquisite and elaborate finishing of the latter.

The general appearance of the Adjunta caves is similar to that of the caves of Ellora; that is, they are mostly low, with a flat roof supported by massive pillars having cushioned capitals; but there is a great deficiency in ornamental carving and fret-work. Some, however, are exceptions to this remark. In most of the caves, to compensate for the want of profuse entaille and sculptures, are paintings in fresco, much more interesting, as exhibiting the dresses, habits of life, pursuits, general appearance, and even features of the natives of India, perhaps, two thousand or two thousand five hundred years ago, well preserved and highly coloured, and exhibiting in glowing tints, of which light red is the most common, the crisp-haired aborigines of the sect of Buddhists, who were driven from India to Ceylon after the introduction of Brahminism.

. . . The Buddhists adore one deity (some peculiarities in whose personification in these caves shall be hereafter noticed); they are monotheists, and their religion is exoteric; while the gods of the present race of Hindus are uncountable. Some speculators in Hindu mythology maintain that the chief temple in all Jain and Buddha caves being arched, shews a posterior date to the flat-roofed excavations of Elephanta [on the west coast], and others appropriated to the followers of Brahma: and, in support of this theory, it is said that the Hindus, previously to the Muhamedan invasion, wereunacquainted with the manner of constructing the arch. But when we consider that these vast excavations must have been hewn out of the living rock, while the Jains were in the plenitude of their power, and long before the persecutions had begun by the followers of Brahma, I think we may safely assert that their antiquity is much greater than that of either the Ellora or Elephanta excavations.

Respecting the antiquity of the Jain or Buddhist religions: in the earliest accounts of India, by Arrian and other authors, and at the period of Alexander's expedition in 327 B.C., the natives are described as having long hair and slender bodies, and as being divided into different castes or tribes. It is therefore pretty evident that the religion of Buddha was then on the decline: for I think that its high antiquity may be satisfactorily proved, both from the paintings and sculptured figures in these excavations; which exhibit traces of the existence of a woolly-haired race, now no where found on the Indian continent; and who, according to the commonly received legend, were persecuted and scattered by the disciples of Brahma; a considerable body of them being driven to Ceylon, from whence they spread the religion of Buddha through Siam, Burma, and China. This persecution is supposed to have arisen from the Buddhist religion (when placed in immediate comparison with the Brahminical) not being suited to the taste of the inhabitants of Hindoostan, who are fond of glitter and shew, and who dazzled by the splendour of the present rites, turned from these plain and unadorned figures of Buddha, to the mysterious Trimurti, and wonder-working Avatárs. From these premises I conceive the age of the caves of Adjunta to be nearer three than two thousand years.

EXAMINATION OF THE CAVES.

The principal excavation, or grand temple, is situated about a hundred and fifty feet from the bed of the nullah, or stream, and on the face of the hill. The magnificent entrance [to Cave 10] is surrounded by scattered jungle and brushwood, and is particularly striking; being a lofty portico, somewhat resembling those of Caneri [Kanheri] and Carli [Karli, south-east of Elephanta]. In the centre of the portico is an immense horse-shoe arch, on each side of which there stand colossal janitors, ten or twelve feet in height, and with curled hair. At the request of the guide we approached with great caution; and on coming under the arch he pointed to the roof, from which a number of wild bees (*apis rufa*) had suspended their pendant hives. We were careful not to disturb them, or they would have soon deprived us of the use of our visual organs, here so much required.

We proceeded to the interior. On looking round, I found myself in a lofty and well-lighted hall, which may be about twenty-five or thirty feet in height, instead of the low caves with flat ceilings, as in the other parts of the hill. This is a well-aired chamber, and in many respects similar to the high coved excavation of Carli, or to what is commonly termed the carpenter's cave at Ellora. The form of the arch is however different. In the Carli cave the roof bears a close resemblance to the high-pointed gothic arch. It is ribbed with teak wood, so as to fit the cove, and is attached to the stone by wooden nails or teeth. In the Ellora caves, stone ribs supply the place of the teak ones of Carli; but the Adjunta cave has a Saxon or (nearly) semicircular roof, without ribs of any sort. Two rows of hexagonal pillars run along the sides of the cave, and behind them is a passage. The entablature of the pillars is without ornament, and the pillars themselves are quite plain. Many of them are broken off, and have fallen on the floor.

Opposite to, and about fifty feet from the entrance, at the farther extremity of the cave, is what is called, in descriptions of the caves of Carli, &c. a circular temple; but which I consider to be nothing more than the *rostrum* from which the *Rhahans*, or Buddhist priests, recited prayers and delivered homilies to the assembled congregation in the hall. . . .

The stone hemisphere, then, probably served the purpose of a pulpit. It rests on a pedestal, somewhat larger than the hemisphere, surmounted by a square block, in shape resembling the capital of a pillar. In Ellora the *figure* of the deity, of gigantic dimensions, is placed on a seat in front of this hemisphere of stone; *but* in this cave it is omitted. In the gallery, or passage behind the pillars, are fresco paintings of Buddha and his attending supporters, with *chowrees*★ [original footnote: ★ Painted sticks, to which are attached the tails of the Thibet cow; used to drive away flies.] in their hands. The thickness of the stucco is about a quarter of an inch. The colours are very vivid, consisting of brown, light red, blue, and white: the red predominates. The colouring is softened down, the execution is bold, and the pencil handled freely; and some knowledge of perspective is shewn. The figures are two feet and a half or three feet in height. . . . That these excavations served for the retirement of some monastic society, does not, I think, admit a doubt. Adjoining the large caves are several cells with stone bed-places, which, in all probability, were the abodes of the devotees: and in many there are springs of clear water.

The other caves which I visited are all flat-roofed, and generally in excellent preservation. The fetid smell, however, arising from numerous bats (*vespertilio noctula*) which flew about our faces as we entered, rendered a continuance inside, for any length of time, very disagreeable. I saw only one cave with two stories or tiers of excavated rock [Cave 6]. In it the steps from the lower apartments to the upper had been destroyed by the *Bheels*....

The paintings in many of the caves represent highly interesting and spirited delineations of hunting scenes, battles, &c. The elephants and horses are particularly well drawn. On the latter two men are often seen mounted. Ram and cock-fights I observed in one of the excavations. The spears are peculiar, having three knobs near the head; and there was an instrument resembling a lyre with three strings. [In Cave 17] I observed something like a zodiac; but not at all resembling the celebrated one of Dendera [in Egypt]. The pillars, in most of the caves, resemble the cushion-capitaled ones of Elephanta. In one I saw a pair of fluted pilasters: and fluting is supposed to have originated in Greece, to prevent the spears from slipping off the columns.

THE FIGURE OF THE GOD.

Buddha is commonly represented of gigantic size, in a sitting posture, and holding the little finger of his left hand between the forefinger and thumb of his right.... The statues of Adjunta are well proportioned, but deficient in anatomical expression: for among nations of luxurious habits the figure of Apollo supersedes that of Hercules. The figures, however, are in perfect unison with the other sculpture of the caves. The features are of African cast; with curled hair and prominent lips. The chiselling of the hair resembles strings of beads. In some, the hair is concealed by a tiara; in others by a conical crown, like that of the Burman Buddha: in most a drapery, similar to that on the head of the Egyptian sphynx, adorns the head. The lobes of the ears are elongated and hang upon the shoulders. The vestment, in many of the figures, consists only of a shoulder band, which may be the origin of the *zenaar*, or sacred string of

the present race. In the left foot of the largest figure is a square hole, which is not observed in any of the others.

After making a few hasty sketches of the lower caves, and the most interesting objects in them, I consumed some time in unavailing attempts to reach some apparently well-preserved caves higher up on the hill. We clambered up on our hands and knees, till stopped by a precipice; and not having ropes, we were unable to reach the caves from above: we therefore gave up the attempt in despair, and after we had partaken of a slight repast, and a *chilum* had been smoked in one of the best lighted and finest excavations, we returned to the horses, and rode back to the town of Adjunta.

Though it was but a rapid and unsatisfactory glance (unsatisfactory in as much as my time was limited, from my leave being nearly expired) that I had of these imperishable monuments of antiquity,

> Quæ non imber edax non aquilo impotens
> Possit diruere, aut innumerabilis
> Annorum series,★

yet I was highly delighted with my excursion; and although many are the caverned temples which I have explored, and many which I wish to revisit, yet to none would I sooner return than to those of Adjunta....

Royal Military College, Sandhurst,
August 1828.

★ Horace, *Odes*, III, 30: 'Exegi monumentum', lines 3–5:
[I have achieved a monument more lasting
than bronze, and loftier than the pyramids of kings,]
which neither gnawing rain nor blustering wind
may destroy, nor innumerable series of years,
[nor the passage of ages. . . .]

(translation by W.G. Shepherd in *Horace: the Complete Odes and Epodes with the Centennial Hymn*, Harmondsworth, 1983)

Extracts from *THE JOURNAL OF THE ROYAL ASIATIC SOCIETY OF GREAT BRITAIN AND IRELAND*, Vol. 8 (1846), pp. 30–56:

Art. II.—*On the Rock-Cut Temples of India*, *by* James Fergusson, Esq.

Read, December 5, 1843.

There are few objects of antiquarian research that have attracted more attention from the learned in Europe, than the history and purposes of the Cave Temples of India, but if we except the still unexplained antiquities of Mexico, I know none regarding which so little that is satisfactory has been elicited, or about which so many, and such discordant opinions exist: and while the age of every building of Greece and Rome is known with the utmost precision, and the dates of even the Egyptian monuments ascertained with almost as much certainty as those of mediæval cathedrals, still all in India is darkness and uncertainty . . .

. . . in the various journeys I undertook I was enabled to visit almost all the rock-cut Temples of India, from those of Cuttack and Mahavellipore [Mamalapuram] on the east coast, to those of Ellora and Salsette on the western side; and there are few buildings or cities of importance in India which I have not at one time or other been able to visit and examine. I had besides the advantage, that as all my journies were undertaken for the sole purpose of antiquarian research, I was enabled to devote my whole and undivided attention to the subject, and all my notes and sketches were made with only one object in view, that of ascertaining the age and object of these hitherto mysterious structures. Whereas, most of those who have hitherto written on the subject, though drawing and writing better than I can pretend to do, have only visited the caves and temples incidentally while travelling on other avocations; and none that I know of, have been able to embrace so extensive a field of research as I have.

I hope, therefore, it will be understood, that the following remarks are not offered as the result of much learning or deep research, but simply as the practical experience of an architect in a favourite branch of his study.

In a short paper as the present is intended to be, it will be impossible to enter into all the arguments that may be urged for and against the various disputed points of Indian and Buddhist chronology; . . . That I may, however, be understood in the following remarks, I will state here the principal conclusions I have arrived at regarding the religion of India, without entering on the grounds on which they were formed, or the reasoning by which they are supported.

The first is, That prior to the advent of the present Buddha, a Brahmanical religion existed in the country, a deistical fire-worship, very unlike the present religion bearing that name. That contemporary with this a Buddhistical religion also existed, differing but little from the other, probably two forms of the same religion. The former has entirely perished, and Buddhism, as we now know it, owes its origin to Gotama Buddha, the son of Suddodana; and was either an entirely new form given to the pre-existing religions, or what is more probable, a reform of both, meant probably to amalgamate the two. It could not however have differed much from the Brahmanism of those days, as we find the kings and people changing backwards and forwards, from one to the other, without difficulty or excitement; and in the description of the Greeks and in native records, we often find it difficult to distinguish between the one and the other.

2nd. It appears also certain that the correct date for Sakya Buddha obtaining Nirvana was 543 B.C. The principal authority opposed to this date are the trans-Himalayan chronologies, which generally concur in placing him about five hundred years earlier. They, however, contain their own refutation, (though I have never observed it pointed out,) inasmuch as they all place the event in the reign of Ajatasatta, and place Asoka little more than one hundred years after. Whereas, the date of the latter is perfectly ascertained to be about 250 B.C.; and of the former, not many years from when the Ceylonese authorities place it.

3rd. That from the time of Asoka till the destruction of the Andhra dynasty of Magadha in the beginning of the fifth century, Buddhism was the principal religion in the north of India, though in the south it never seems to have obtained a permanent footing, where the Brahmanical religion still prevailed, and during the time of Buddhist supremacy in the north, that form of it was elaborated which flowing back on the parent country exists in the form we now find it.

With regard to the antiquity of the monuments, all that is here necessary to state is, that the oldest relics of whose existence I am aware are the Laths, bearing the inscriptions of Asoka, dating from the middle of the third century B.C. I am not aware of the existence of any cave anterior to, or even coeval with these, nor of any structural building whose date can reach so high as the first centuries of our era.

I may also state that it appears quite evident that the Buddhists were the earliest cave diggers, and that it is not difficult to trace the connection of the whole series from "the earliest abode of Bauddha ascetics" at Nagarjuni, to the Kylas at Ellora; but as the principal object of the present paper is to point out this connection, I will not enlarge upon it more in this place; but in order to be understood, I must, before proceeding to describe particular caves, say a few words on the subject generally, to point out the different classes into which they are divided, and consequently, explain the names I shall apply to them throughout.

As far as my knowledge of the cave temples of India extends, the whole may be classified under the following heads.

First, Vihara, or Monastery Caves.
1st, The first subdivision of this class consists of natural caverns or caves slightly improved by art; they are as might be assumed the most ancient, and are only found appropriated to religious purposes in the older series of Behar [Bihar] and Cuttack; and though some are found among the western caves, their existence there appears to be quite accidental.

The second subdivision consists of a verandah, opening behind into cells for the abode of the priests, but without sanctuaries or images of any sort. The simplest form of this class consists of merely one square cell with a porch, several instances of which occur in the Cuttack series; sometimes the cell is nearly thirty feet long, as in the Ganesa Gumpha . . . ; and at Ajunta in the oldest Vihara there, the arrangement is further extended by the verandah opening into a square hall, on three sides of which the cells are situated.

In the third subdivision of the Vihara caves, the last arrangement is further extended by the enlargement of the hall, and the consequent necessity of its centre being supported by pillars; and in this division besides the cells that surround the hall, there is always a deep recess facing the entrance, in which is generally placed a statue of Buddha with his usual attendants, thus fitting the cave to become not only an abode for the priests, but also a place of worship. At Baug, the statue of Buddha is replaced by the Daghopa; but this is I believe a solitary instance of its existence in a Vihara cave.

To this division belongs by far the greatest number of Buddhist excavations. The most splendid of them are those at Ajunta; though the Dherwarra, at Ellora, is also fine; and there are also some good specimens at Salsette, and I believe Junír.

The Second class consists of Buddhist Chaitya Caves.

These are the temples, or if I may use the expression, the churches of the series, and one or more of them is attached to every set of caves in the west of India, though none exist in the eastern side.

Unlike the Viharas, the plan and arrangement of all these caves is exactly the same; and though the details and sculpture vary with the age in which they were executed, some strong religious feeling seems to have attached the Buddhists to one particular form for their places of worship.

In the Viharas, we can trace the progress from the simple cavern to the perfect monastery, but these seem at once to have sprung to perfection, and the Karli cave, which is the most perfect, is, I believe, also the oldest in India. Had the style been gradually elaborated in the rock, from the imperishable nature of such monuments we could not fail to have discovered the earlier attempts; but besides this, there are many reasons that I shall notice in the proper place, which lead me to suppose that they are copies of the interior of structural buildings; and it is not one of the least singular circumstances attached to their history, that no trace of such buildings exists in India, nor, I believe, in Ceylon, nor in the Buddhist countries beyond the Ganges.

All these caves consist of an external porch, or music gallery, an internal gallery over the entrance, a centre aisle which I will call the nave, (from its resemblance to what bears that name in our churches,) which is always at least twice the length of its breadth, and is roofed by a plain waggon vault; to this is added, a semi-dome terminating the nave, under the centre of which always stands a Daghopa or Chaitya.

A narrow aisle always surrounds the whole interior, separated from the nave by a range of massive columns. The aisle is generally flat-roofed, though sometimes in the earlier examples it is covered by a semi-vault.

In the oldest temples the Daghopa consists of a plain circular drum, surmounted by a hemispherical dome crowned by a Tee [square capital], which supported the umbrella of state. In the earlier examples this was in wood, and as a general rule it may be asserted, that in these all the parts that would be constructed in wood in a structural building, are in wood in the caves; but in the more modern caves all those parts, such as the music gallery outside, the ribs of the roof, the ornaments of the Daghopa, the umbrella of state, &c., are repeated in the rock, though the same forms are preserved. In front of the more modern Daghopas there is always a sculptural niche containing a figure of Buddha with his attendants; this may have existed in wood in the more ancient, and consequently have disappeared, but I am rather inclined to think it is a modern innovation.

These two classes comprehend all the Buddhist caves in India.

The Third class consists of Brahmanical *caves*, properly so called.

In form many of them are copies of, and all a good deal resemble the Buddhist Vihara, so much so as at first sight to lead to the supposition that they are appropriations of Buddhist caves to Brahmanical purposes. On a more intimate acquaintance however with them, many points of distinction are observed. The arrangement of the pillars, and the position of the sanctuary, is in no instance the same as in a Vihara; they are never surrounded by cells, as all Viharas are, and their walls are invariably covered, or meant to be, with sculpture; while the Viharas are almost as invariably decorated by painting, except the sanctuary. The subjects of the sculpture of course always set the question at rest.

The finest specimens of this class are at Ellora and Elephanta, though some good ones exist also on the Island of Salsette, and at Mahavellipore.

The Fourth class consists of rock-cut Models of structural Brahmanical temples, or, as I will call them, "Pseudo-structural temples." To this class belong the far-famed Kylas at Ellora, the Sivite temple at Doomnar, and the Ruths at Mahavellipore. Except the last, which are cut out of isolated blocks of granite, these temples possess the irremediable defects of standing in pits, which prevents them being properly seen, and the side of which being of course higher than the temples, crushes them and gives them an insignificant appearance; and though they are not the least interesting, they are in worse taste and worse grammar than any of the preceding ones.

The Indra Subha group at Ellora should perhaps form a Fifth class, as it cannot in strictness be brought under any of the above heads; but it is difficult to decide whether they are Brahmanical or Jaina; if the former, they belong to the third class, if the latter, they must be classed with what in reality form the

Fifth class, or true Jaina caves, which, without this splendid auxiliary are few and insignificant, though there are some tolerable ones at Khandagiri in Cuttack, and in the southern parts of India; and in the rock of the fort at Gualior [Gwalior], there are a number of colossal figures of one or the other of the [twenty-four] Thirthankars cut in the rock, with sometimes, though not always, a small screen left before them, which thus forms a small chamber. Some of them are sitting, some standing, and many of colossal dimensions, from thirty or forty feet high; the whole however is of rude bad sculpture, and the date about, or rather subsequent to the eleventh or twelfth century of the Christian era.

Before proceeding to describe particular caves, I may also mention here, that in speaking of Buddhist Chaitya caves, I have used terms borrowed from the names given by antiquarians to the different parts of Christian churches, because in form and arrangement they so exactly resemble the choirs, more particularly of the Norman churches of the eleventh and twelfth centuries, that no confusion can arise from my doing so, and I know not where to look for other terms, that would apply to them, and be intelligible. . . .

The first series of caves I will mention are those in Behar, which I have not myself seen, as from the descriptions I had read of them I knew that they possessed no great architectural magnificence, and I was not aware, till too late, that these were perhaps some of the oldest caves in India; and their locality, too, in the very birth-place of Buddhism, gives them an interest which no other series possesses, and which certainly would have led me to visit them, had I been as fully aware of it then, as I have since become; for situated in the immediate neighbourhood of Rajagriha, the capital of India at the time of Buddha's death, and where the first convocation was held, and in the neighbourhood of the capital of Asoka, they occupy the locality from which we might expect more of interest than from any series in India. . . .

As far as our researches have yet gone these are the most ancient caves in India; and I know of no other caves which from their locality, their form, or their inscriptions, can compete with them in this respect. . . .

The next series in antiquity, and one of the most interesting in India, though one of the least known, are the caves of Khandagiri, situated about twenty miles from Cuttack, and five from Bodaneswar [Bhubaneswar]. There are here two small but picturesque and well-wooded hills of a coarse-grained sandstone, very rare in that neighbourhood, which seem from a very early period to have been a sport held particularly sacred by the Buddhists; and though no caves exist here that can vie in size or magnificence with those of Western India, there are a greater number of authentically ancient caves here, than in any other series, and the details of their architecture are of a higher class than any other I am acquainted with.

. . . The caves on the Udyagiri (hill of the rising sun) are entirely Buddhist, and of a very early and pure type; those on the other hill, the Khandagiri, are much later, and principally Jaina. . . .

. . . as it would take up too much space here to enter into all the arguments that might be urged on this head, I shall content myself with stating, that I think the balance of evidence inclines to a date about two hundred years before Christ, and that cannot be very far from the truth.

The other caves on this hill have all inscriptions in the Lath character, and therefore may all be safely assigned to a date anterior to the Christian era, and probably between that and the date above given. The only apparent exception is that on the Ganes Gumpha, which is in the Kutila character of the tenth century of our era; but the cave in which it is engraved is so entirely of the same character as the rest, both in architecture and sculpture, that it cannot be assigned to a different era, and the inscription must be considered as marking its conversion to the Brahmanical faith. All the larger ones consist of a pillared verandah, of from six to ten feet in width, the length varying with the number of cells which open into it from behind, these being generally about six feet wide. In the Thakoor cave, (the large one above alluded to, to which I could not obtain admittance,) the colonnade is the longest here, being fifty-five feet in length, with wings extending at right angles to it in front.

In the Ganes Gumpha, which is perhaps the most beautiful of the series, the verandah is thirty feet long by six feet wide, and seven in height; there are four doors which open from it into the inner excavation, which is seven feet six inches deep, and of the same length as the verandah. In this instance it is not divided into separate cells.

The sculpture on this cave is superior to anything I have seen in India, and I wish much it could be cleaned and casts taken of it. It consists of a frieze at the back of the verandah, broken into two compartments by the heads of the doors. . . .

The only sculpture I am aware of that resembles it in India, is that of the Sanchi Tope, near Bhilsa, and it resembles European art more than any other. There are no gods, no figures of different sizes, nor any extravagance; everything is in keeping and in good taste.

. . . On the Khandagiri the caves are much less interesting, being all of an evidently later date. One called Lelat Indra Kesari ka Noor, probably was excavated by that prince, and its date therefore will be the beginning of the seventh century; it is an excavation of no great extent, and it is not easy to make out from the very unfinished state in which it has been left, for what purpose it was designed, being extremely unlike all the others of the series.

As Lelat Indra, however, was a devout worshipper of Siva, and built, or at least finished the great temple at Bobaneswar, it was probably intended to be a Brahmanical cave, like those at Ellora or Elephanta; his Rani, however, was a follower of Buddha, and this may have been her work.

Close to it is the largest cave on this hill; like most others, it consists of a verandah with pillars and a long apartment parallel to it, to which has recently been added an outer verandah of masonry plastered and painted. In this cave are sculptured the images of the twenty-four Thirthankars, and their female energies, which are probably coeval with its excavation, and at one end an image of the monkey-god Hanuman, though he probably is of a later date; he was however too well covered with red paint for me to make out from the style of sculpture to what age he belonged.

. . . One of the most singular features in all the Buddhist caves here, is the total absence of all images of Buddha, and indeed of any apparent object of worship; a circumstance which alone would, I conceive, be sufficient to place them in a higher antiquity than any series in Western India; for it is tolerably certain that the adoration of images, and particularly of that of the founder of the religion, was the introduction of a later and more corrupt era, and unknown to the immediate followers of the deified.

Whatever sculpture is used in these caves, and they contain some of a very high class, is purely ornamental, and has no reference either to the worship of Buddha, or to the purposes for which these caves were excavated.

. . . There are not, as far as I am aware of, any other caves on the eastern side of India, certainly none of any importance, except those at Mahavellipore . . .; and we must therefore step at once to the western side, where they exist of a size and magnificence totally unknown on the eastern side. I have not been able to visit all the caves myself, but I have examined those of Ajunta, Karli, Salsette, Doomnar, Ellora, Elephanta, and Mahavellipore. The caves of Nasik, Junir, and Baug, I have not been able to visit, but from all I could learn on the spot, the two first mentioned series contain no type not seen at Karli, Ellora, or Salsette, while the latter are so similar to those at Ajunta, that though extremely numerous, and no doubt interesting, I am not aware of them offering any thing of a new or distinctive character.

In attempting to describe so many caves, it would be desirable, if possible, to adopt some mode of classification by which to connect so many dissimilar objects. The most desirable would certainly be a chronological one, describing each cave according to its date; but their ages are so imperfectly ascertained, that this would at present, I fear, only lead to confusion; and as each series extends through several hundred years, some nearly a thousand, and consequently, they were contemporary one with another, no succession can be made out between the different series. I shall therefore describe those I have visited in the order in which I have named them above, placing Ajunta first because it is the most perfect and complete series of Buddhist caves in India, without any admixture of Brahmanism . . .

After crossing the valley of the Taptee from the north, you approach a ghát of some five or six hundred feet in height, supporting the table-land of the Dekkan. The upper line of the ghát is flat and regular and the wall, if I may use the expression, tolerably even except in some places where it is broken by ravines, which extend for a considerable way into the table-land above. It is in one of these ravines that the caves of Ajunta are situated. The entrance to the ravine is nearly half a mile in width, but is gradually narrower as you wind up it, till it terminates in a cascade of seven falls, called the sat koond; the lowest fall may be one hundred feet high, the others together one hundred more.

Immediately below the fall the ravine makes a sudden turn to the right, and it is in the perpendicular cliff forming the outer side of the bend, and facing the koond, that the caves are situated; the whole series extending, as nearly as I can guess, about five hundred yards from north to south-east.

The most ancient are situated about one-third of this distance, or about one hundred and fifty yards from the most northern end, and are the lowest down in the rock, not being above thirty or forty feet above the bed of the torrent, while to the north they rise to about eighty feet, and at the southern extremity they rise to about one hundred or one hundred and fifty feet; the extreme excavations however are at this end unapproachable, in consequence of the ledge of the stratum, which formed the terrace of communication along the whole series, having fallen away, and left the face of the cliff perpendicular for its whole height, which is as nearly as I could estimate about three hundred feet.

Names have been given to some of the caves, but these are neither very appropriate nor well understood, and as the local cicerone who accompanied me the first day gave the same name to different caves at different times, and, I believe, invented others when his memory failed him, I adopted the surer plan of using numbers; and, beginning at the northern end, or that lowest down the stream, called the first cave number one, and so on to twenty-seven, which is the last accessible cave at the south-eastern extremity; and as this plan can

lead to no confusion, I shall now follow it.

According to this arrangement, the ninth, tenth, nineteenth, and twenty-sixth, from the north end, are Chaitya or Daghopa vaulted caves, without cells; the rest are all Viharas, or Monasteries, with cells and flat roofs.

The lowest down and the most ancient, are the twelfth and eleventh; the first-named is the plainest cave of the series, being entirely without pillars, and there is no sanctuary or image, nor, apparently, any visible object of worship; indeed, its only ornament consists of seven horseshoe canopies on each side, four of which are over the doors of the cells, the other three merely ornamental; they are very similar to those at Cuttack, and under them is a reeded string course, similar to that used in those caves, and which I have not observed any where else except there and at the great Karli cave; indeed, it resembles the caves in the Udyagiri in almost every respect, except it being square, thirty-six feet seven inches each way, while those at Cuttack are all longer than their depth. The front would have afforded the best means of identification, but unfortunately it is entirely removed by the rock above giving way; I searched earnestly for inscriptions, but could only find one on the inner wall, in a character slightly modified from that on the laths, and, therefore, probably written early in the Christian era; but it does not, from its position, seem to be at all integral, or to form a part of the original design, and therefore would not fix the date even if deciphered.

The next cave to the north, number eleven, is not quite so large, being only thirty-seven feet ten inches, by twenty-eight feet six inches; it is very similar in some respects to the last, but has four pillars in the centre supporting the roof.

This is, probably, one of the earliest instances of the introduction of pillars for such a purpose, and though they are clumsily used here, the example is interesting, as it was to the extended use of them, that we owe all the magnificence of the modern Vihara; the window on each side of the door is divided into three lights, by two pillars standing on each cill. The sanctuary is not finished, and, indeed, seems to have been an afterthought; but there are antelopes, lions, and a boy in an attitude of prayer, sculptured on the wall in the very best style of art, and evidently coeval with those of the Ganesa Gumpha at Cuttack; the walls have been stuccoed and painted, but the paintings are so much destroyed as to be scarcely distinguishable; I could discover no inscription on any part of it.

The next two caves to these on the north side, numbers ten and nine, are two Daghopa caves, almost counterparts of one another, except that the first is very much the largest, being ninety-four feet six inches in depth, and forty-one feet three inches wide, while the other measures only forty-five feet by twenty-three feet.

The largest one has, or rather had, twenty-nine pillars surrounding the nave; they are plain octagons, without capital or base, and have been covered with stucco and painted; thirteen of them are fallen, leaving large gaps in some places, and the outer screen is entirely gone. Like all Daghopa caves, it has a ribbed roof. In some caves, the ribbing is in stone, in others, as at Karli, it is in wood. This cave combines both methods, the aisles being of stone, while the nave has been ornamented with wood, which has entirely disappeared, except some of the battens and pins that fastened it to the rock, and the footings for the ribs, which are sunk to some depth in the rock.

The Daghopa is plain and solid, without any ornament, except the square capital or tee on the top, but there can be no doubt that it was once richly ornamented, probably in wood, for which some mortices remain; and that it was crowned, as at Karli, by three umbrellas.

The whole of this cave has been covered with stucco and painted, and many of the smaller paintings on the pillars, and in the panels of the roof of the aisles remain, consisting of figures of Buddha and his disciples in various attitudes, rosettes and other ornaments; but owing to the ruined space of the front, the rain apparently has beat in, and destroyed the larger subjects. There are several inscriptions painted on the plaster, and though none remain sufficently entire to be transcribed, yet sufficient remains to show, that the characters are those that were used subsequently to the Christian era.

On the exterior face, however, of the cave, but very high up, is an inscription of some length in the pure Lath character, which would at once give an antiquity to the excavation of about 100 or 200 B.C., as far as such evidence can be relied on.

The smaller cave had only twenty pillars surrounding the nave, similar to those in the other; eight of them are broken, but at the entrance there are four pillars of a different form and richer detail. Of its paintings but little remains, except in the inner wall, where they are still tolerably entire. In this circle I found two inscriptions painted on the stucco on the walls; the first under a figure seated on a chair, with the fore finger of the left hand touching that of his right, the second under a Daghopa, painted also on the wall. And on the south side of the cave, opposite the first, there was a third inscribed in a panel under another figure, seated in a chair, but so defaced, that I could only see that it was in the same character as the other two; its existence, however, appeared to me very valuable, from its position as an integral portion of the design which it forms a part of, and if its age can be determined, it will show the period at which the paintings were executed. I have not myself much difficulty in assigning it, . . . to the second or third century of our era.

The eighth cave from the end is merely a natural cavern, without any inscription or object of interest; and the seven that precede it, are so modern, that I would prefer going back to number thirteen, and continue to describe them as they occur from this point towards the southern extremity, as I shall thus preserve something like the succession of dates in which they were excavated, without the confusion that would arise from selecting here and there.

Thirteen is only a small cave with two cells, and has nothing remarkable about it.

Fourteen is a large unfinished cave under thirteen, and apparently meant as an under story to it; only the first line of the pillars in the interior is hewn out, and left in a rough state. The verandah pillars, however, are finished, and are of an unusual form, from being merely square piers with plain bands.

Fifteen is a plain square cave, but filled up with mud and debris nearly to the roof, so that there is considerable difficulty in effecting an entrance, and only its general plan can be made out.

Numbers sixteen and seventeen are the two finest Viharas of the series, and apparently belong to, and were excavated at the same time, with nineteen, which is the best finished Chaitya cave of the series; to these may be added the one beyond number twenty, as they all seem of the same age, and the four together form the most interesting group of the Ajunta caves. There are two long inscriptions on the external faces of sixteen and seventeen, which probably contain something of their dates and history; I did not, however, attempt to copy either, and my opinion of their age, therefore, rests entirely on their architectural details and their position in the series; I believe them to have been excavated between the fourth and sixth century after Christ, but more probably about the latter date.

Sixteen is a square cave, sixty-seven feet six inches wide, and sixty-five feet two inches deep, exclusive of the sanctuary; the centre hall is surrounded by twenty pillars, generally of an octagon form, the sides of which are adorned in painting with something like a Roman scroll, alternating with wreaths of flowers.

All the details of its architecture are particularly good and elegant, more so than any other cave in this series; there are no side chapels, but eighteen cells surrounding the great hall. The figure in the sanctuary is seated with his feet down; some of the paintings are tolerably entire and extremely interesting, though not so much so as those in the next cave; the swords in the soldier's hands are shaped something like the Nepalese Kookry [*kukri*], and the shields are of an oblong form.

Seventeen, generally called the Zodiac cave, very much resembles the last described in almost every respect. Its dimensions are sixty-four feet by sixty-three feet, and it has twenty pillars disposed as in the other; it is not, however, so lofty, and the details of the pillars are by no means so graceful or elegant as in number sixteen. The paintings, however, are much more entire, and though the colours in some places are a good deal faded, the subjects can generally be made out.

On the right hand wall, as you enter, a procession is painted. Three elephants issuing from a portal, one black, one red or rather brown, and the third a white one, which seems the principal one of the group; showing how early arose the predilection for these animals, which still exists among the Burmese and Siamese of the present day. Chattahs and flags are borne before them, and men with spears, swords, and shields make up their retinue.

On the back wall is a hunting scene, in which a maned lion, powerfully and well-drawn, forms the principal object of attraction; there are also deer and dogs, and men on horseback and on foot without number.

In the verandah to this cave are some singularly interesting paintings; at one end a circular one, which I at first took for a zodiac, though, on further examination, I gave up the idea; its centre is divided in eight compartments, and the outer circle into sixteen or seventeen. Each of these compartments are crowded with small figures, but what the subject is I could not make out.

Over the door are eight figures sitting cross-legged; the first four are black, the fifth fairer, the next still more so, the last fair and wearing a crown. It may be remarked, that there are more black people painted in this cave than in any of the others: the women, however, are generally fair, and the men all shades, from black to a European complexion. The roof is painted in various patterns, not at all unlike those still existing in the baths of Titus, though in an inferior style of art. I had not time, even if I had had the ability, to copy these interesting paintings, and I fear any one who now visits them will find that much that I saw has since disappeared.

The style of these paintings cannot of course bear comparison with European painting of the present day; but they are certainly superior to the style of Europe during the age in which they were executed: the perspective, grouping, and details are better, and the story better told than in any paintings I know of, anterior to Orgagna and Fiesole. The style, however, is not European, but more resembles Chinese art, particularly in the flatness and want of shadow; I never, however, even in China, saw anything approaching its perfection.

I looked very attentively at these paintings, to try and discover if they were fresco paintings, or merely water colours laid on a dry surface; but was unable to decide the point: the colour certainly is in some cases absorbed into the plaster, and I am inclined to think they may have been painted when it was first laid on, and consequently moist; but I do not think it could have been done on the modern plan of painting each day all the plaster laid on that day.

Eighteenth Merely a porch of two pillars, apparently the commencement of an excavation, or of a passage or entrance to

The Chaitya cave, number nineteen, which is more remarkable for the beauty and completeness of its details than for its size, being only forty-six feet four inches, by twenty-three feet seven inches in width. Seventeen pillars surround the nave, all of which are very richly ornamented, and above them is a band occupying exactly the same position as a triforium would in a Christian church, and occupied here with niches containing alternately figures of Buddha sitting cross-legged, and standing. The roof is ribbed in stone, but the most interesting feature is the Daghopa, which has here the three umbrellas in stone rising till they touch the roof; in front of the Daghopa is a figure of Buddha, standing. The exterior of this cave is as rich as the interior, and though damaged in some parts, by the rocks falling from above, the injury is less than in most others, and very little labour would free the lower part from the accumulated materials, and display entire one of the most perfect specimens of Buddhist art in India; but one that I must not dwell on longer, as I feel that, without drawings, I should be unable to convey to others any correct impression of its beauties or details.

Twenty. The last of this group is a small Vihara of singular plan, twenty-eight feet two inches wide, by twenty-five feet six inches deep, with two cells on each side. There is no internal colonnade, but the roof is supported by advancing the sanctuary about seven feet into the hall, and making its front consist of two columns

in antis. There is also a verandah in front, with an apartment at each end. Its paintings are almost entirely obliterated, except those on the roof, and these consist of frets and flowers, not otherwise interesting than merely as showing its connection with the Viharas sixteen and seventeen. There is an inscription on one of the pillars of the verandah, but very much obliterated, and apparently not integral.

Before proceeding further in this direction we must return back to the seventh and sixth from the north, and which, though scarcely coeval with the last group described, are certainly later than those first mentioned, and as certainly earlier than the group which succeeds, and which closes our list; but whether they are antecedent to numbers sixteen and twenty, or slightly posterior to them, I am unable to decide.

Number seven is merely a large verandah, sixty-three feet four inches in length, by thirteen feet seven inches in breadth, with the cells opening at the back of it, something in the manner of the Cuttack caves; the front line of the verandah is broken by the projection of two porches of two pillars each, which are here particularly interesting, as they are extremely similar to the pillars at Elephanta, and those in the Doomar Lena at Ellora, and therefore probably not far distant in date. There is also a chapel with two pillars at each end.

To the left of the sanctuary are five cross-legged figures, each seated on a lotus, and a lotus between each; on the right, two cross-legged and seven standing figures, the centre lotus of each series supported by figures with snake canopies. Within the sanctuary, on each side, are two large and one smaller figures, and two men sitting cross-legged, and having chowries in their hands. On the step are sixteen figures of disciples seated cross-legged.

Number six is the only two-storied cave at Ajunta. The upper story has twelve pillars, octagons changing into plain squares at top and bottom, and with bold bracket capitals, not painted but sculptured with figures of Buddha. At first I thought this a Jaina cave, and tried to find the twenty-four thirthankars in some place, but was unsuccessful; the series consist of sixteen, eight, four, and are apparently of disciples, as none had the emblems by which the thirthankars are usually recognised.

The case is fifty-three feet square, the aisles nine feet wide. The lower story is of the same dimensions as the upper, and of the same plan, except that four additional pillars have been introduced in the centre; they are all plain octagons, changing to sixteen sides, with pilasters to each row. Seven of these only are standing, nine having fallen down, owing to the inferiority of the rock in which they are cut, and also to water entering from above, and rotting the stone; the whole cave has a dismal and ruinous look not common here; and it is also without sculpture, having apparently depended entirely on painting for its decoration. The pillars in front of the sanctuary are of the same Elephanta character as those of the last-mentioned cave.

There now only remains to be described the last group of these caves, consisting of the first five from the north, and the last seven at the other extremity; they are all so nearly of the same age, that I am quite unable to discriminate between them, and all evidently the last excavated here. They are singularly unlike any other caves or structural buildings I am acquainted with, and I had consequently less means here than with the others of coming to a satisfactory conclusion regarding their dates; if, however, we assume the last group to have extended to the sixth or seventh century of our era, these must range between that period and the tenth, after which time I conceive no Buddhist caves were excavated in India, and we cannot therefore be far wrong in placing them in the eighth and ninth centuries.

As I cannot fix their succession, I may as well begin with number one, and passing over those already described, proceed to twenty-seven, the last visited.

The first that commences, or rather ends, the series on the north, is a very handsome vihara cave, with a fine verandah ninety-eight feet in length, and a chapel at each end, the hall is sixty-four feet square, adorned with twenty pillars three feet in diameter, richly carved, and with bracket capitals. The cave is a good deal filled up with mud, but, notwithstanding, the paintings are tolerably

entire, and some of them very interesting; though both they and the details of the architecture are small and frittered away, when compared with the two first-described groups.

The second is a twelve-pillared cave . . .; it is in very good preservation, and the paintings, particularly on the pillars, are tolerably perfect. In the sanctuary there is a statue, of course of Buddha, and a chapel on each side of it, at the end of the aisles. In the one on the north are two most portly, fat figures, a male and female: in the south one, two male figures, occupying a like position. Who they were meant to represent I could not make out, for they were quite strangers to me.

The third is a very fine bold cave, and one of the largest viharas of the series, but does not appear to have been quite finished; the colonnade in the centre consists of twenty-eight pillars, (the only instance I know of such magnificence,) disposed in four ranges of eight pillars each, counting the angular ones in each line; the pillars, generally bold octagons eleven feet in circumference; the whole hall is ninety-one feet square; the aisles twelve feet two inches wide, which is also the width of the verandah. This cave never having been finished does not appear ever to have been painted. It is now so dreadfully infested with bats that it is almost impossible to stay in it any length of time, and I had not the courage to explore its cells; as, however, I found nothing of interest in any of the others, I do not suppose there was much to regret here.

The fourth cave is situated higher up in the face of the rock, and as there is no path to it, I did not discover its existence till the day I was leaving the place, when I saw it from the opposite side of the ravine which I had scrambled up to in a wild-goose chase, to look for the city of Lenapore, having been delighted with its name, and convinced, in spite of the assurance of my guides, that it must contain something of interest; it was, however, "vox et præterea nihil [literally, 'a voice and beyond that nothing', according to Plutarch a Spartan saying coined in reference to a plucked nightingale]."

The fifth was so choked up with mud, that it was almost impossible to see what it was, further than that it had been a square cave of no great dimensions.

We must now return to cave number twenty, the last described towards the south.

Leaving it you proceed for some distance along the ledge, which, owing to a torrent coming over here during the rains, is more than usually ruined, and the path in some places very narrow and dangerous; and as I had to traverse this several times in the middle of the day at the end of March. I suffered extremely, not only from the heat of the sun, but from the reflection from the rocks, which were heated like an oven.

Having passed this, however, you arrive at the twenty-first cave from the north end, a large vihara, fifty-two feet six inches deep, by fifty-one feet six inches in width. It is similar in almost every respect of plan, style, and execution, to the cave above described as number two. It is, not, however, quite finished, as the pillars of the sanctuary are only hewn rough out of the rock, and many of the details are left incomplete. Its paintings are now nearly obliterated, except on the wall on your left hand as you enter, where there still exists a large figure of Buddha, of a black complexion, or at least very dark, and with red hair, and attended by black slaves. There are several ladies introduced into the composition, but notwithstanding the blackness of their companions, they are here, as in most other caves, represented with complexions almost as fair as Europeans. There is a small chapel with two pillars in antis, on each side, as well as at each end of the lateral aisles. The verandah has fallen down, but the chapels at each end remain, with the pilaster which terminated the colonnade at each end, showing its dimensions and depth.

As I before remarked, the execution of this cave, as well as of number two, is decidedly inferior to that of the intermediate ones; not indeed in richness and quantity of ornament, but in style. There is a weakness in the drawing of the details, and the ornaments are crowded and cut up in a manner that gives a tawdry and unsatisfactory appearance to the whole; very unlike the bold magnificence of those of an earlier age. To use a comparison drawn from the architecture of our own country, they bear the same relation to numbers sixteen, seventeen, and twenty, as the Tudor architecture does to the pure Gothic of the Third Edward.

The twenty-second is a small cave only seventeen feet square, without pillars, excepting two rough-hewn ones in front of the sanctuary, in which is a figure of Buddha seated, with his legs down.

The twenty-third is another vihara of twelve pillars, very similar in all respects to numbers two and twenty-one; it has, however, been left in a very unfinished state, without even an image in the sanctuary, or indeed anywhere else, and there exists no trace of painting that I could detect in any part. Its dimensions are fifty-one feet by fifty-one feet eight inches.

Number twenty-four is the pendant in the series to number three, and would have been one of the finest had it been finished; but merely its general form and dimensions have been made out. Only one pillar has been completely sculptured, and one side of the colonnade exists as a wall with slits in it. It was intended to have been a twenty-pillar cave; the centre hall would have been about forty-three feet square, and the whole about seventy-four feet each way. The details of sculpture and style are of the same class as two, three, and twenty-one, but much more pains appears to have been taken with their execution, and on the whole they are richer than those above alluded to, if it is fair to judge by what is visible; for besides that so little has been executed, the cave is now half filled with mud. The verandah has been completed, but three out of its six columns are broken, and the others much injured.

This cave is particularly interesting as showing the whole process of excavation, from its commencement to the finishing of the details, some parts having been left in every stage of advancement. The rock (amygdaloidal trap) in which they are cut is of a soft, coarse texture, so that the labour of excavation could not have been so great as is generally supposed; indeed, I am very much inclined to believe that this mode of excavating was the cheapest and least laborious by which buildings of this class could be erected. If the stones were quarried so as to be of use for building purposes at the same time, it certainly would be so; but that does not seem to have been the case here, as all the rough work appears to have been done with the pick-axe.

Twenty-five. A small rude vihara cave, with a verandah of ten pillars.

Twenty-six is the fourth vaulted or chaitya cave of this series, and decidedly the most modern. In general plan it is very similar to number nineteen, but its dimensions exceed the former very considerably, the whole width being thirty-six feet three inches, that of the nave seventeen feet seven inches, and the total length sixty-six feet one inch. Its sculptures, too, are far more numerous and more elaborate, indeed, more so than in any other cave of the series; but they are very inferior both in design and in execution, so much so that if other proof were wanting this alone would be sufficient to stamp this at once as one of the latest, if not the last executed cave of Ajunta.

The Buddha on the front of the Daghopa is seated with his feet down.

The walls of the aisles are entirely covered with sculpture, principally figures of Buddhas or disciples, of all sizes, and in every Buddhist position. Among others in the south aisle is one twenty-three feet long, reclining at all his length, being the attitude in which they prepare to receive nirvana (beatitude); above him are an immense host of angels, awaiting apparently his arrival in heaven, and one beating most vigorously a big drum.

The fat figures with judges' wigs, who do duty as brackets, have here four arms, which is the only instance I am aware of in these or any other Buddhist caves, of such a piece of Hinduism.

The details of the pillars, particularly those of the verandahs, are of precisely the same character as all those of this group, but their details are worse executed here, than in any of the others.

There are two inscriptions on the outside of the cave apparently integral, one under a figure of Buddha on your left as you enter, the other is much broken but more distinct, upon your right. The character used in them belongs to the ninth or tenth century of the Christian era.

The twenty-seventh cave is a small square vihara without pillars, and the sanctuary only commenced, and the whole left in a very unfinished state; the front has entirely crumbled away, so that its dimensions can scarcely be ascertained; it was, however, about forty feet in width.

There are one or two caves beyond this, but the ledge having fallen away, they are quite inaccessible. From the ruined state of their fronts, and the debris that has accumulated before them, I was unable to guess either at their size or state of progress; judging, however, from the last caves visited, there cannot be much worth seeing in them, and indeed, I am not quite sure that what I took for caves were not holes, or shadows thrown by masses of rock.

I have been more particular in describing this series than any other, partly because I am not aware that any detailed account of them has been given to the public to which I could refer, and partly because they are in some respects the most interesting series of Buddhist caves in India. They cannot, indeed, boast of a chaitya cave like Karli, but the viharas here are more splendid than anywhere else; they are more entire, and are the only caves that retain much of their original painting and decoration. They also are purely a Buddhist series, and almost every change in cave architecture can be traced in them during a period of about one thousand or twelve hundred years, which is nearly the term during which the religion flourished in its native land; and they thus form a sort of chronometric scale, which I found extremely useful in my attempts to ascertain the ages and dates of caves in other series, none of which are so complete as this one. . . .

SELECT BIBLIOGRAPHY
(ARRANGED CHRONOLOGICALLY)

GENERAL

Annual Report[s] of the Archaeological Department of His Exalted Highness the Nizam's [of Hyderabad] *Dominions*, Calcutta, especially: *1917–18* (1919), pp. 11–12; *1918–19* (1920), pp. 7–8; *1919–20* (1922), pp. 3–4; *1920–21* (1923), pp. 14–16; *1921–22* (1926), pp. 7–9; *1924–25* (1926), pp. 7–8; *1936–37* (1939), pp. 25–30

MĀRG (Modern Artists and Architects Research Group, Bombay): vols. IV (1947–48); IX (1956); XX (1967) – various articles on Ajanta

OTHER BOOKS, ARTICLES ETC.

J.E. Alexander, 'Notice of a visit to the cavern temples of Adjunta in the East-Indies', *Transactions of the Royal Asiatic Society of Great Britain and Ireland*, II (1830), pp. 362–70

J. Fergusson, 'On the rock-cut temples of India', *Journal of the Royal Asiatic Society of Great Britain and Ireland*, VIII (1846), pp. 30–92

Bhau Daji, 'Ajunta inscriptions', *Journal of the Bombay Branch of the Royal Asiatic Society for 1861–62 and 1862–63*, VII (1865), pp. 53–74

J. Burgess, 'Rock-temples of Ajanta', *Indian Antiquary*, III (1874), pp. 269–74;
——, *Notes on the Bauddha Rock-temples of Ajunta, their Paintings and Sculptures and on the Paintings of Bagh Caves, modern Bauddha Mythology, etc.*, Archaeological Survey of Western India, 9 (Bombay, 1879)

James Fergusson and James Burgess, *The Cave Temples of India* (London, 1880), esp. pp. 280–349

James Burgess and Bhagwanlal Indraji, *Inscriptions from the Cave-temples of Western India*, Archaeological Survey of Western India, 10 (Bombay, 1881)

James Burgess, *Report on the Buddhist Cave Temples and their Inscriptions*, Archaeological Survey of Western India, IV (London, 1883)

E.B. Cowell and R.A. Neil, *The Divyavadana* (Cambridge, 1886)

E.B. Cowell (ed.), *The Jataka* I–VI (Cambridge, 1895–1907; Indian ed., New Delhi, 1990)

H. Kern (ed.), *The Jataka-mala by Aryasura* (Boston, MA, 1891)

H. Kern, *Manual of Indian Buddhism* (Strassburg, 1896)

J. Griffiths, *The Paintings in the Buddhist Cave-Temples of Ajanta, Khandesh (India)*, 2 vols., (London, 1896–97)

J. Fergusson, *History of Indian and Eastern Architecture*, revised, edited and enlarged by J. Burgess and R. Phené Spiers, 2 vols. (London, 1910), esp. I, pp. 125–208 (concerning rock-cut caves, including those at Ajanta)

Lady Herringham, 'The paintings (frescoes) of the Ajanta caves', *Journal of Indian Art*, XV (1913), pp. 56–60

Lady Herringham (with introductory essays by various members of the India Society), *Ajanta Frescoes: being reproductions in colour and monochrome of some of the caves at Ajanta . . .*, (London, 1915)

A. Foucher, 'Preliminary report on the interpretation of the paintings and sculptures of Ajanta', *Journal of the Hyderabad Archaeological Society for 1919–20* (Bombay), pp. 50–111

A.K. Coomaraswamy, *History of Indian and Indonesian Art* (Cambridge, MA, 1927)

V. Goloubew, 'Documents pour servir à l'étude d'Ajanta – les peintures de la première grotte', *Ars Asiatica*, X (Paris and Brussels, 1927)

Stella Kramrisch, *The Vishnudharmottara (Part III)*, (Calcutta, 1928)

Balasaheb Pant Pratinidhi, *Ajanta* (Bombay, 1932)

R.S. Wauchope, *Buddhist Cave Temples of India* (Calcutta, 1933), pp. 96–105

G. Yazdani, 'Notes on frescoes discovered at Ajanta', *Annual Bibliography of Indian Archaeology for the year 1932*, VII (Leyden, 1934), pp. 31–32

Stella Kramrisch, *A Survey of Painting in the Deccan* (London, 1937), pp. 3–69

Benjamin Rowland, *The Wall-Paintings of India, Central Asia & Ceylon* (with an introductory essay by A.K. Coomaraswarny), Boston, MA, 1938

G. Yazdani, *Ajanta. The Colour & Monochrome Reproductions of the Ajanta Frescoes Based on Photography*, 4 vols. (London, 1930–55)

Percy Brown, *Indian Architecture (Buddhist and Hindu)*, (Bombay, 1942)

Madanjeet Singh, *India – Paintings from the Ajanta Caves* (UNESCO, World Art Series, New York, 1954)

Benjamin Rowland, *The Art and Architecture of India: Buddhist, Hindu, Jain* (Harmondsworth, 1956), pp. 137–42

Ajanta Paintings (Lalit Kala Akademi [National Academy of Art] and Department of Archaeology, Government of India, New Delhi, 1956)

The Ajanta Caves, with introduction by Benjamin Rowland, Mentor-UNESCO Art Book (New York, 1963)

Vasudev Vishnu Mirashi, *Inscriptions of the Vakatakas*, Corpus Inscriptionum Indicarum, V (Ootacamund, 1963), pp. 103–29

Debala Mitra, *Ajanta: Painting, Sculpture, Architecture* (New Delhi, 1964)

Madanjeet Singh, *Ajanta: Painting of the Sacred and the Secular* (New York, 1965);

——, *The Cave Paintings of Ajanta* (London, 1965)

A. Ghosh (ed.), *Ajanta Murals* (Archaeological Survey of India, New Delhi 1967)

Philippe Stern, *Colonnes Indiennes d'Ajanta et d'Ellora* (Paris, 1972)

Karl Khandalavala, *The Development of Style in Indian Painting* (Bombay, 1974)

Sheila L. Weiner, *Ajanta: Its place in Buddhist Art* (Berkeley, CA, 1977)

C. Sivaramamurti, *Chitrasutra of the Vishnudharmottara* (New Delhi, 1978)

Dieter Schlingloff, *Studies in the Ajanta Paintings, Identifications and Interpretations* (Delhi, 1987)

Ratan Parimoo, Deepak Kannal, Shivaji Panikkar, Jayaram Poduval and Indramohan Sharma (eds.), *The Art of Ajanta, New Perspectives*, 2 vols. (New Delhi, 1991)

Dieter Schlingloff, *Ajanta Paintings* (Delhi, 1991)

Amina Okada (with photographs by Jean-Louis Nou), *Ajanta* (Paris, 1991; Indian ed., Delhi, 1995)

Walter M. Spink, *Ajanta. A Brief History & Guide* (Asian Art Archives, University of Michigan, Ann Arbor);

——, 'The Archaeology of Ajanta', *Ars Orientalis*, XXI (1991)

Ancient India: Land of Mystery (Alexandria, VA, 1994)

INDEX